2024

Realschulabschluss
Original-Prüfungsaufgaben und Training

Hessen

Englisch

STARK

© 2023 Stark Verlag GmbH
20. ergänzte Auflage
www.stark-verlag.de

Das Werk und alle seine Bestandteile sind urheberrechtlich geschützt. Jede vollständige oder teilweise Vervielfältigung, Verbreitung und Veröffentlichung bedarf der ausdrücklichen Genehmigung des Verlages. Dies gilt insbesondere für Vervielfältigungen, Mikroverfilmungen sowie die Speicherung und Verarbeitung in elektronischen Systemen.

Inhalt

Vorwort
Hinweise und Tipps zur schriftlichen Realschulabschlussprüfung

Übungsaufgaben

Übungsaufgabe 1 1
Übungsaufgabe 2 18
Übungsaufgabe 3 34
Übungsaufgabe 4 50

Schriftliche Abschlussprüfungsaufgaben

Abschlussprüfung 2017 .... E 2017-1
Abschlussprüfung 2018 .... E 2018-1
Abschlussprüfung 2019 .... E 2019-1
Abschlussprüfung 2020 .... E 2020-1
Abschlussprüfung 2021 .... E 2021-1
Abschlussprüfung 2022 .... E 2022-1

Abschlussprüfung 2023 .... www.stark-verlag.de/mystark
Sobald die Original-Prüfungsaufgaben 2023 freigegeben sind, können sie als PDF auf der Plattform MyStark heruntergeladen werden (Zugangscode vgl. Umschlaginnenseite).

Sollten nach Erscheinen noch wichtige Änderungen an der Realschulabschlussprüfung vom Kultusministerium bekannt gegeben werden, findest du aktuelle Informationen dazu auch auf unserer Plattform MyStark.

Autorinnen und Autoren:
Brigitte Katzer und Gerhard Philipp (Übungsaufgaben),
Redaktion (Übungsaufgaben, digitale Kurzgrammatik)

Hördateien 🔊

Übungsaufgabe 1: Part One: Booking a hotel room/
Booking a flight
Übungsaufgabe 1: Part Two: Part-time jobs
Übungsaufgabe 1: Part Three: Applying for a job
Übungsaufgabe 2: Part One: The pardoning of the Thanksgiving turkey/
What about a Batmobile?
Übungsaufgabe 2: Part Two: What do you think about Halloween?
Übungsaufgabe 2: Part Three: Integrated prom
Übungsaufgabe 3: Part One: America returns into space/
Italian nun wins "The Voice of Italy"
Übungsaufgabe 3: Part Two: Five-star hotel or wilderness?
Übungsaufgabe 3: Part Three: An interview with Jennifer Brown
Übungsaufgabe 4: Part One: Announcement on board/
Traffic update
Übungsaufgabe 4: Part Two: What's on your plate?
Übungsaufgabe 4: Part Three: An interview with Amy Smith
Listening Comprehension 2017
Listening Comprehension 2018
Listening Comprehension 2019
Listening Comprehension 2020
Listening Comprehension 2021
Listening Comprehension 2022
Listening Comprehension 2023

Hinweis: Die MP3-Dateien kannst du über den Zugangscode freischalten, den du in der Umschlaginnenseite findest.
Sprecher*innen der Hörverstehenstexte (Übungsaufgaben):
Daniel Beaver, Clare Gnasmüller, Daniel Holzberg, Rees Jeannotte, Barbara Krzoska, Jennifer Mikulla

Die Hintergrundgeräusche stammen aus folgenden Quellen: freesound, pacdv, soundsnap

Vorwort

Liebe Schülerin, lieber Schüler,

Prüfungen sind oft mit einer gewissen Unsicherheit verbunden: Man ist sich nicht sicher, ob man genug und das Richtige gelernt hat und wie man die ungewohnte Prüfungssituation bewältigen wird. Eine gute Vorbereitung ist hier der Schlüssel zum Erfolg. Mit dem vorliegenden Buch kannst du dich anhand einer Vielzahl von Aufgaben optimal auf die zentrale Abschlussprüfung im Fach Englisch an der Realschule vorbereiten.

– Die **Übungsaufgaben** erlauben es dir, gezielt auf die Prüfung hinzuarbeiten. Sie sind genau im Stil der Abschlussprüfung aufgebaut. So kannst du trainieren, wie man an Prüfungsaufgaben herangeht und wie man sie erfolgreich löst.

– Anhand der vom hessischen Kultusministerium gestellten **Original-Prüfungsaufgaben der letzten Jahre** kannst du sehen, wie die offizielle Prüfung angelegt ist. Wenn du die Übungsaufgaben gewissenhaft durchgearbeitet hast, kannst du bestimmt auch die Original-Prüfungsaufgaben ohne Probleme lösen.

Außerdem umfasst dieser Band **digitale Inhalte**, auf die du mit deinem persönlichen Zugangscode (vgl. Umschlaginnenseite) über unsere Online-Plattform **MyStark** zugreifen kannst:

– Die aktuellen **Original-Prüfungsaufgaben der Abschlussprüfung 2023** findest du auf MyStark als PDF-Datei.

– Die **Hörverstehensdateien** zu allen Übungs- und Prüfungsaufgaben stehen dir als **MP3-Dateien** zur Verfügung.

– Neben vielen Aufgaben im Buch findest du das Symbol für „**interaktive Aufgabe**". Diese Aufgaben kannst du auch am Computer oder Tablet bearbeiten. Das Online-Training auf MyStark enthält darüber hinaus auch Aufgaben zur Wiederholung von Wortschatz und Grammatik.

– In der **digitalen Kurzgrammatik** werden für die Prüfung wichtige grammatische Themen knapp erläutert und an Beispielsätzen veranschaulicht. Hier kannst du schnell suchen, wenn du dir bei der Grammatik unsicher bist.

– Zu einigen grammatischen Strukturen, mit denen erfahrungsgemäß viele Schüler*innen Schwierigkeiten haben, gibt es zusätzlich **Lernvideos**.
Ein weiteres Video zeigt dir außerdem, wie du mithilfe von **Lernstrategien** deinen **Wortschatz** erweitern und festigen kannst.

Zu allen Videos gelangst du über die Plattform MyStark oder über folgenden Link bzw. QR-Code:

http://qrcode.stark-verlag.de/lernvideos-englisch-1

- Mit der Web-App „**MindCards**" kannst du am Smartphone hilfreiche Wendungen wiederholen, die vor allem für den Prüfungsteil *Text Production* sehr nützlich sind.

  Über folgende Links gelangst du zu den MindCards:
  https://www.stark-verlag.de/mindcards/writing-1
  https://www.stark-verlag.de/mindcards/speaking-1

  Du kannst auch einfach die folgenden QR-Codes scannen:

  Writing   *Speaking*

Der **Lösungsband** zu diesem Buch ist unter der Bestellnummer D06150L erhältlich. Darin findest du zu allen Aufgaben von unseren Autorinnen und Autoren ausgearbeitete Lösungsvorschläge, mit denen du deine Lösungen überprüfen kannst. Außerdem gibt es viele Bearbeitungshinweise, die dir beim richtigen Beantworten der Aufgaben helfen.

Viel Spaß beim Üben und viel Erfolg in der Prüfung!

Hinweise und Tipps zur schriftlichen Realschulabschlussprüfung

1 Ablauf der Prüfung

Allgemeines

Die Übungen in diesem Buch entsprechen in ihrer Struktur der realen Prüfung. Nachdem du den Prüfungsraum betreten hast, wirst du zu Beginn der Prüfung die Aufgaben und eine ausreichende Menge an Schreibpapier (Reinschrift- und Schmierpapier) ausgehändigt bekommen. Alle ausgeteilten Blätter müssen am Ende der Prüfung wieder abgegeben werden, unabhängig davon, ob du sie benutzt hast oder nicht. Die Lösung für die *Text Production* kann nur dann gewertet werden, wenn sie auf Reinschriftpapier geschrieben ist.

Bearbeitungszeit

Vor Beginn der Bearbeitungszeit hast du 15 Minuten Zeit, dich mit der Abschlussarbeit vertraut zu machen, und dann noch einmal ca. 15 Minuten, um allgemeine Fragen zu stellen. Die anschließende Bearbeitungszeit beträgt 135 Minuten.

Erlaubte Hilfsmittel

Du darfst während der Prüfung ein zweisprachiges Wörterbuch benutzen, aber kein elektronisches Wörterbuch.

2 Inhalte und Schwerpunktthemen

Der Aufbau der Prüfung ist stets ähnlich. Bei den Themen handelt es sich um typische Situationen aus dem Alltagsleben, z. B. Sport und Freizeit oder Umwelt und Schulleben. Die Prüfung besteht aus folgenden Teilen: *Listening Comprehension, Reading Comprehension, Use of Language* und *Text Production*.

Im Prüfungsteil **Listening Comprehension** hörst du zuerst kurze Texte (z. B. Nachrichtenmeldungen oder Durchsagen). Danach werden dir meist eine Umfrage (oder ein bzw. mehrere Dialoge) und ein längeres Interview vorgespielt. Bevor du die Texte hörst, erhältst du etwas Zeit, um den entsprechenden Teil des Aufgabenblattes durchzusehen. Damit hast du die Möglichkeit, dich auf die Bearbeitung der Aufgaben zu konzentrieren, während die Texte ein erstes Mal vorgespielt werden. Höre dabei ganz genau zu. Nach einer kurzen Pause wirst du die Texte ein zweites Mal hören. Während der Pause und während du die Texte noch einmal hörst, kannst du deine Lösung überprüfen und noch fehlende Angaben ergänzen.

In der **Reading Comprehension** erhältst du mehrere Texte, die du durchlesen sollst und zu denen im Anschluss Aufgaben zu bearbeiten sind.

Im Prüfungsteil **Use of Language** musst du zwei verschiedene Aufgaben bearbeiten: *Mediation* (Sprachmittlung) und *Words and structures*.

Den Schluss der Prüfung bildet die **Text Production**. Dort werden drei Themen vorgeschlagen. Du kannst ein Thema auswählen und musst dazu einen ungefähr 150 Wörter langen Text in englischer Sprache verfassen.

Nach der *Listening Comprehension* steht es dir frei, welchen Teil der restlichen Aufgaben du als Nächstes bearbeiten möchtest. Es wird keine Reihenfolge vorgeschrieben. Teile dir deine Zeit gut ein, damit du dir am Ende alles noch einmal durchlesen kannst.

3 Aufgabenarten

Typische Aufgabenformate im Bereich **Listening Comprehension** sind:
- *Multiple Choice*: Hier kreuzt du jeweils die zutreffende Aussage an.
- *Matching:* Matching-Aufgaben können in vielfältiger Form vorkommen. Es können dir z. B. einige Satzanfänge vorgegeben werden, denen du das richtige Satzende zuordnen musst. In einem anderen Aufgabenformat ist eine Auswahl an Aussagen vorgegeben. Deine Aufgabe ist es dann, anhand der Äußerungen die Gedanken den Sprechern zuzuordnen. In der Regel können nicht alle Alternativen zugeordnet werden.
- *Tabelle*: Deine Aufgabe ist es, die fehlenden Informationen in einer Tabelle zu ergänzen.

Im Bereich **Reading Comprehension** kommen häufig folgende Aufgabenformate vor:
- *Matching*: Deine Aufgabe ist es hier, mehrere thematisch ähnliche Texte einander zuzuordnen oder verschiedenen Textabschnitten vorgegebene Überschriften zuzuordnen.
- *Multiple Choice*: Hier kreuzt du jeweils die zutreffende Aussage an.
- *Questions on the text*: Hier musst du Fragen zum Text beantworten.

Der Prüfungsteil **Use of Language** besteht aus zwei Teilen:
- *Mediation*: Hier geht es um die Übertragung von Informationen vom Englischen ins Deutsche und umgekehrt. Typische Aufgabenformate sind:
  – Als Dolmetscher musst du zwischen einem englisch- und einem deutschsprachigen Gesprächspartner vermitteln; du musst dabei sinngemäß Aussagen und Fragen von einer Sprache in die andere übertragen.
  – Du musst einem vorgegebenen englischen Text (z. B. Broschüre, Website oder E-Mail) Informationen entnehmen, diese auf Deutsch wiedergeben und anschließend englische Formulierungen oder Fragen zu diesem Thema erstellen.
- *Words and structures*: In diesem Prüfungsteil wird dein Wissen um Wortschatz und Grammatik überprüft. Es handelt sich um einen Lückentext, bei dem du per Multiple Choice die richtigen Wörter für die Lücken auswählen musst.

Im Teil **Text Production** musst du selbst einen kurzen Text verfassen.
Folgende Arten von Texten können hier z. B. von dir verlangt werden:
- eine Geschichte (zu einem Bild)
- ein kurzer Bericht oder Artikel oder eine Meinungsäußerung
- Briefe oder E-Mails
- ein Tagebuch- oder Blogeintrag

In der Regel bekommst du in Stichpunkten vorgegeben, welche inhaltlichen Elemente in deinem Text enthalten sein sollen.

4 Allgemeine Tipps zur schriftlichen Prüfung

Für eine erfolgreiche Abschlussprüfung ist es wichtig, dass du rechtzeitig mit der systematischen Vorbereitung beginnst. Wenn du im Jahr vor der Prüfung schon Probleme in Englisch hattest, dann mache bereits Anfang des Jahres einen **Plan**, wie du die Arbeit gut schaffen kannst.

Versuche in der Prüfung immer die **Ruhe** zu bewahren und dich nicht verunsichern zu lassen, wenn du eine Antwort nicht gleich weißt.

Achte darauf, dass du die Zeit in der Prüfung sinnvoll einteilst. Ideal ist es, wenn du am Ende noch einmal Zeit hast, die komplette Prüfung in Ruhe durchzulesen. So kannst du Flüchtigkeitsfehler vermeiden. Die richtige **Zeitplanung** kannst du bei der Vorbereitung mit diesem Buch üben: Nimm dir genau die Zeit, die dir auch in der Prüfung zur Verfügung steht und übe unter den **realen Bedingungen** (z. B. ohne Handy und ohne größere Pausen). So gewöhnst du dich an die Zeitvorgaben und an die Prüfungssituation.

Ein Hinweis zur **Bewertung:** Um die höchste Punktzahl in der *Listening Comprehension* zu erhalten, kommt es hauptsächlich darauf an, den **Inhalt** richtig zu erfassen und wiederzugeben. In einer Aufgabe, bei der du selbstständig formulieren musst, erhältst du einen Punkt für jede verständliche und sinngemäß richtige Antwort. Halte dich aber an die Vorgaben. Die Nennung mehrerer Aspekte pro Frage ist möglich, doch es wird kein Punkt vergeben, wenn ein Aspekt falsch ist. Sprachliche Fehler führen nicht zum Punktabzug, solange der Sinn erkennbar ist.

In der *Text Production* werden der Inhalt, die Struktur (der Aufbau), der Wortschatz und die grammatischen und syntaktischen Strukturen jeweils extra bewertet.

Hessen Realschule – Englisch
Übungsaufgabe 1

Listening Comprehension – Transcripts

Hello, this is the listening exam. I am going to give you the instructions for the test. There are three parts to the listening exam. At the start of the listening texts you will hear this sound: ◀
You may write down your answers at any point during the listening exam.

Part One

In part one you will hear two short dialogues. You will hear the dialogues twice. Before listening to the texts, you will have 20 seconds to read the tasks. You now have 20 seconds to read the tasks for dialogue one.
You are now going to hear dialogue one for the first time. After a short break, you will hear the dialogue again. ◀

Dialogue 1: Booking a hotel room

RECEPTIONIST: The Old Waverley Hotel, Edinburgh. This is Lewis Breckenridge speaking. How may I help you?
SOPHIE: Hello. This is Sophie Burns. I'd like to book a hotel room for my parents for their silver wedding anniversary. It's a surprise.
RECEPTIONIST: Oh, wow, your parents have been married for 25 years! What a great idea to send them to Edinburgh on a romantic trip. Can you give me the dates, please?
SOPHIE: Yes, isn't it? Ah, it's from the 15th to the 18th August.
RECEPTIONIST: OK. I'll just check if we've got any vacancies at that time – you know, August is usually really busy because of the Fringe Festival. Just a moment, please …
Ah, you're extremely lucky. We've just had a cancellation. There's only one room left.
SOPHIE: That's fantastic. What type of room is it and how much does it cost?
RECEPTIONIST: It's a beautiful large double room with a fantastic view of Edinburgh Castle. Unfortunately, prices are up in August, so it's £165 per night for the room.
SOPHIE: Oh … I can't afford that.
RECEPTIONIST: Ah, I see. Well, just to let you know: we've got a special offer for online bookings for the winter months. So if it was possible for your parents to travel, say, in December, you could book dinner and full English breakfast for them in our restaurant at full price and you'd just have to pay £1 per person for their room per night!
SOPHIE: That sounds great. I'll think about it. Thank you so much for the information.
RECEPTIONIST: You're very welcome. Bye.
SOPHIE: Bye-bye.

You now have 20 seconds to read the tasks for dialogue two. You are now going to hear the second dialogue for the first time. After a short break, you will hear dialogue two again. ◀

Dialogue 2: Booking a flight

MILLIE: Good afternoon. This is Millie Croft speaking. How may I help you?
GRACE: Hello. This is Grace Arnold. I booked flights with your airline about two hours ago. I just got the bill for three tickets via email. However, the price on the invoice is $30 higher than the one given online.
MILLIE: I see. Where are you travelling to?
GRACE: We're flying to Atlanta.
MILLIE: Do you have the booking number at hand?
GRACE: Yes. It's WYEZ – 3566.
MILLIE: WYEZ – 3566. OK. Let me just have a

look at your booking … The price I see here is $ 532 in total.
GRACE: Exactly. But when I clicked OK, it was $ 30 less. How is that possible?
MILLIE: That's strange indeed … As I see it, you've already booked your seats.
GRACE: Yes, I did. I've got a service card of the airline, so it should be free of charge.
MILLIE: You're right there, but you booked seats with extra leg space and that's $ 10 per person.
GRACE: Oh, I did that by mistake. Can you change the seats?
MILLIE: No problem at all. Just wait a moment …

Part Two

In part two you will hear an interview. Listen to reporter Poppy Mitchell talking to some high school pupils about their part-time jobs. You will hear the interview twice. Before listening to the interview, you will have 40 seconds to read the task. You now have 40 seconds to read the task.
You are now going to hear the interview for the first time. After a short break, you will hear the interview again. ◄

Interview: Part-time jobs

REPORTER: Good morning, ladies and gentlemen. This is Poppy Mitchell and I'm reporting live from Forrester High School. Today I'm trying to find out what kinds of jobs pupils do to earn some extra money.
My first interview partner here is seventeen-year-old Lexi. Lexi, do you have a part-time job?
LEXI: Yes, I do. I'm a babysitter. I usually work every Friday and Saturday afternoon, and sometimes in the evenings, too. It's the best job I can imagine, because it never gets boring. I love kids and playing with them. I look after our neighbours' children. They're two, five and eight years old.
MARC: My name's Marc and I'm sixteen. I don't have a part-time job right now. I used to work for a pizza delivery service for a few months and I really liked it. It was my job to buy the ingredients at the markets, but I also had to work in the kitchen or even deliver the pizzas. My parents made me quit two weeks ago, because my marks are too bad in Maths.
LEO: I'm Leo, I'm sixteen, too, and I'm a Maths tutor. If you want, I can help you improve your marks, Marc. My rates are affordable for everyone.
I do private and group tutorials and the feedback I get is really good, because I'm patient and I always prepare my own material. I want to become a Maths teacher in the future.
FREYA: Hi, I'm Freya and I've been delivering newspapers in our neighbourhood since I was thirteen years old. That is the minimum age children are allowed to work, you know! Some of my friends say they'd never want to do my job, but I really like it. For me, it's relaxing. I spend lots of time outside and I can daydream. It's perfect after a long day sitting in a classroom.
RILEY: Hi there, I'm Riley and I love animals. That's why I work at the local animal shelter at the weekends and in the summer. It's volunteer work, so I don't get paid, but I don't mind. My job's still important.
LUCAS: My name's Lucas and I've never had a part-time job. And I wouldn't want one. Why should I make an effort if I get everything I want anyway? You know, both my parents are successful lawyers and they always work long hours. Money isn't a problem.
HOLLIE: But don't you feel lonely sometimes, Lucas? I'm Hollie and although my parents could probably afford to give me more pocket money, I'm proud to be earning money of my own. It's a great feeling that I don't have to ask for permission when I want to buy something. Two years ago, I started to make my own jewellery and sell it online and at markets. Especially my earrings are a great success. I'm always very happy when I see someone wearing a piece I've made.
REPORTER: Thank you all for answering my questions honestly. I wish you all the best for your future.

Part Three

> In part three you will hear a job interview with Eileen O'Hara, who has applied for a job as a member of the cabin crew of an important Irish airline. You will hear the interview twice. Before listening to the interview, you will have 30 seconds to read the task. You now have 30 seconds to read the task. You are now going to hear the interview for the first time. After a short break, you will hear the interview again. ◀

Interview: Applying for a job

PERSONNEL MANAGER: Hello, Miss O'Hara, my name is Frank Foster. I'm the manager of the Human Resources Department of our airline. Please take a seat.
APPLICANT: Thank you.
MANAGER: Can I offer you something to drink?
APPLICANT: I'm fine, thank you.
MANAGER: OK. So, you want to be a member of our cabin crew. Tell me something about yourself.
APPLICANT: Well, I'm 25 years old and I was born in Dublin. When I finished my hotel training in Limerick, I worked in a big hotel in London for three years. I like to travel and read. I speak German fluently and a little French.
MANAGER: You speak German?
APPLICANT: Yes. My mother's German and she's always spoken German to me, while my father has always spoken English.
MANAGER: So you grew up with both languages. Excellent. Now why do you want to work for our airline?
APPLICANT: Every time I flew with your airline, I felt safe and well looked after on board. And all the cabin crew were so friendly. So all in all, my experiences have given me a really positive impression of your company. But of course, I did some research as well. Your airline is a leading airline in Europe. I found some impressive information about future projects you have planned, and I was also impressed with the history of the airline. Another reason is that you already have some destinations in Germany, and you plan to expand on the German market. I'd like to put my German skills to good use.
MANAGER: The job of a flight attendant is very challenging physically. You must be able to stand for a long time; you have to be strong enough to lift heavy hand luggage and push heavy beverage carts. How do you keep fit?
APPLICANT: I love running. Usually, I run about six kilometres three times a week. I also do yoga and weight training once a week.
MANAGER: What are your feelings regarding the lifestyle changes a career as a flight attendant would bring?
APPLICANT: I'm aware that I'd have to travel a lot and that I'd have shift duties. But that wouldn't be a problem to me.
MANAGER: How willing are you to relocate?
APPLICANT: I have no problems with moving to another country within Europe. I could easily imagine living in Paris or Berlin, for example. But, to be honest, I wouldn't want to live outside Europe.
MANAGER: Is there anything you'd like to add, or do you have any questions?
APPLICANT: Yes, I do have a question. I'd like to know where the training centre is and how long the training lasts.
MANAGER: The flight attendant training takes place at our airline training centre here in Dublin and typically lasts seven weeks. The first five weeks are classroom based. In the last two weeks you will put what you've learned into practice on board. Classes are usually made up of between 20 to 40 trainees and run from 8:00 a.m. to 5:30 p.m. You'll be paid for the duration of the course.
APPLICANT: And how soon would you like me to start?
MANAGER: Our next training begins in two months.
APPLICANT: Umm, I'm very interested in the job, so what's the next step for me to take?
MANAGER: You'll hear from us within the next four days and, if we choose you, you should be ready for the training. Thank you for coming. Goodbye.
APPLICANT: Goodbye.

> You can now continue with the rest of the exam. Good luck!

A Listening Comprehension

 Part One

Listen to the dialogues.
Tick (✓) the right sentence endings.

Dialogue 1: Booking a hotel room 4 pts.

a) Sophie Burns wants to book a hotel room
- [ ] near Waverley Station.
- [✓] in Edinburgh.
- [ ] in Breckenridge.

b) Her parents
- [✓] married 25 years ago.
- [ ] know about the trip.
- [ ] married on 15th August.

c) The hotel
- [✓] room costs £ 165 per person.
- [ ] is nearly booked out.
- [ ] room is small, but you can see the castle from there.

d) The hotel
- [ ] has got a special offer only for December.
- [ ] offers breakfast, lunch and dinner.
- [✓] has got a special online offer.

Dialogue 2: Booking a flight 4 pts.

a) Millie Croft
- [ ] wants to fly to Atlanta.
- [✓] works for an airline.
- [ ] wants to complain about a booking.

b) The caller
- [ ] booked a flight three hours ago.
- [ ] has booked plane tickets for $ 30.
- [✓] has booked three tickets.

c) The booking number is
- [ ] WYAZ – 3566.
- [ ] WVEZ – 3566.
- [✓] WYEZ – 3566.

d) The price online and on the bill differs
- [ ] because the caller does not have a service card.
- [ ] because it costs $ 10 to book a seat in advance.
- [✓] because the caller booked more comfortable seats.

Part Two

Interview: Part-time jobs

Listen to the interview. Some pupils are talking about their part-time jobs. Who thinks what? Write the correct letters in the chart.
Be careful: There is one more statement than you need.

7 pts.

A I can relax while I'm working.

B I don't charge too much for my tutorials.

C I don't work because my parents are rich.

D I'm a designer and I'm proud that many people want to buy my handmade things.

E I regularly look after three children.

F I don't get any money for the work I do.

G My job is exhausting, but I still like it.

H I had to give up my job recently.

Lexi	Marc	Leo	Freya	Riley	Lucas	Hollie
	H	B	A	F	C	D

Part Three

Interview: Applying for a job

In part three you will hear a job interview. You will hear the interview twice. Listen to the interview and fill in the missing information in the grid.

10 pts.

Eileen O'Hara's age	
period of time she worked in London	
the language(s) she speaks fluently	
personal experience with the airline (one aspect)	
one reason why the job is physically demanding	
the sport she does more than once a week	
where she would not like to live	
city where the training for new cabin crew takes place	
number of trainees taking part in the training courses	
period of time the airline will get in touch with Eileen	

B Reading Comprehension

1. Airline information

❶ Our company is based in Ireland. We operate both domestic and international flights to and from six Irish cities to the UK, continental Europe, Asia, Australia, the Middle East, North America and Canada. Our main office and our training centre are located in Dublin. Our team consists of 4,000 employees that are all passionate about the job they do. Our fleet comprises 43 planes. We have approximately 10 million passengers per year on board our planes.

❷ Safety is our main concern. We make sure all our staff are highly qualified for their jobs and capable of dealing with all kinds of difficult situations. At the same time, we want to make the flight experience with us special – for every single passenger. We want our passengers to leave the plane with a smile and to look forward to flying with us again.

❸ On our transatlantic flights, it is now possible for you to stay connected: Onboard Wi-Fi enables you to browse the internet, email or text your friends, family or business partners. You simply have to bring your laptop, tablet or smartphone – it's as simple as that. Business class passengers get internet access for free. Passengers in economy class surf for either € 7.95 for one hour or € 14.95 for the entire duration of the flight.

❹ We introduced a new checked baggage policy for inner-European flights a few years ago in order to accommodate our passengers' needs better. It is now possible to choose between four baggage options if you book online – small (up to 15 kilos), medium (up to 20 kilos), large (up to 25 kilos) and extra large (up to 40 kilos). Keep in mind that no single item can be heavier than 32 kilos.

❺ Interested in working as a cabin crew member? We're looking for motivated men and women who like to work in a great team and who are flexible where irregular working hours are concerned. So if you are basically interested in working as a flight attendant, take the time to answer the following questions for yourself:
Do you like to be busy during working hours all the time? Do you stay friendly although you've had a horribly stressful day? Are you punctual and reliable? Are you spontaneous and creative when it comes to solving problems? Can you keep a cool head in difficult situations? Do you like every day at work to be different? Do you like helping people? Can you listen patiently to people's problems? Do you speak English and a foreign language fluently? If you have answered all these questions with "yes", click here to download the application form.

Abschlussprüfung Englisch – Übungsaufgabe 1

You have found the previous information on the website of an airline. Read the text, find the five correct headings, and match them to each paragraph (1–5). There are two more headings than you need.

5 pts.

A	Flight attendants – competent in handling difficult situations
B	Safety and friendliness
C	Qualities of a flight attendant
D	Luggage regulations
E	Basic information on the airline
F	Use of electronic devices prohibited on board
G	Online on board

part of the text	❶	❷	❸	❹	❺
heading					

2. **Angel Air – Cabin Crew (Flight Attendants)**

Location: Dublin Airport	**Status:** Permanent / Full-Time	**Shift Work:** Yes

1 **Job Description**

Representing Angel Air as a member of our cabin crew is a unique experience. Our customers have their own personal needs and requirements. You'll find every day holds a different challenge from the moment you welcome our customers aboard the
5 aircraft; their safety and comfort are your responsibility. You will hold the key to our customers having a fantastic flight and, most importantly, wanting to fly with us again.

Our international air cabin crew are primarily responsible for ensuring passenger safety during a flight. Before a flight, they receive a briefing on the flight details
10 and schedule, and check all cabin equipment, making sure the plane is carrying sufficient supplies.

Before take-off, they greet the passengers, direct them to their seats, ensure luggage is stored safely and give a safety demonstration showing passengers what to do in an emergency.

15 During a flight, the crew serve meals and drinks, and sell duty-free goods. In an emergency, they stay calm, make sure that the captain's instructions are followed and that safety equipment is being used correctly. If a passenger becomes sick, all cabin crew are trained to administer first aid.

Cabin crew are required to complete some paperwork before the end of a flight, including customs and immigration documents, accounts of duty-free sales and meal and drink orders.

Cabin crew will sometimes have to pay special attention to minors (ages 12–15) travelling on their own. However, children under the age of 12 are not allowed on board without a guardian.

Air cabin crew are usually required to live near the airport where they are based. They could be based overseas as international cabin crew. However, we are currently only hiring for our base in Dublin.

Hours and Working Conditions

Hours of work vary greatly. As the airline operates 365 days a year, shifts include weekends, nights, public holidays and religious festivals. The amount of time spent away from home may change from job to job. Delays and cancellations could mean hours are disrupted. Hotel accommodation is provided when away from home base. Conditions on the aircraft are restricted, with a lot of time spent standing or walking. Jet lag may be a problem when crossing time zones, and air cabin pressure may cause fatigue or other health problems. Bad weather can make flying conditions uncomfortable or even dangerous.

Air cabin crew are expected to have a smart appearance and wear our uniform with pride.

Training

Successful interviewees go on a seven-week training course. Areas that will be studied include: safety and emergency procedures, fire fighting, first aid, security and hijack procedures, cabin service and dealing with passengers.

Air cabin crew have to pass regular examinations that test knowledge of safety and emergency procedures to make sure that official first aid requirements are up to date.

The Benefits
- Full-time basic starting salary of € 30,000 per annum
- Holiday entitlement is 30 days
- Opportunities for career advancement

Application Process and Criteria

Applicants have to be at least 18 years old. High standard of written and spoken English and German are required. Other languages will be an advantage.

To apply, complete the online application form, send us copies of your
- passport,
- birth certificate,
- relevant exam certificates,

and include two passport-sized photographs.

The first stage of the selection procedure is a telephone interview.

Read the text and tick (✓) the correct box. 10 pts.

a) The text is
- [ ] an interview about an airline.
- [x] a job offer.
- [ ] a story about an airline.
- [ ] a newspaper article about Angel Air.

b) Cabin crew
- [ ] have to be from Dublin.
- [ ] will get a short-term contract.
- [x] have to make sure the passengers are safe and feel comfortable on board.
- [ ] can also work part-time.

c) After take-off, cabin crew
- [ ] check the cabin equipment.
- [ ] make sure the passengers' hand luggage is stored away safely.
- [ ] give a safety demonstration.
- [x] offer the passengers something to eat and drink.

d) Angel Air is looking for flight attendants
- [ ] for their only base outside Ireland.
- [ ] for all their bases.
- [ ] only for their Irish bases.
- [x] only for their base in Dublin.

e) The airline
- [ ] does not operate on religious holidays.
- [ ] gives flight attendants heavy discounts on duty-free products.
- [ ] wants flight attendants to be proud of their looks.
- [x] operates all year round.

f) Flight attendants do not have to deal with
- [x] eleven-year-olds travelling alone.
- [x] dangerous flying conditions.
- [x] irregular working hours.
- [ ] jet lag and other health problems.

g) The airline
- [ ] offers applicants one week of training.
- [x] pays all the cabin crew members € 30,000 per year.
- [ ] asks their cabin crew to take tests on safety regularly.
- [ ] does not organise hotel accommodation on layovers.

h) Flight attendants
- [ ] are trained in first aid, cabin service and German.
- [x] can take 30 days off per year.
- [ ] are trained in security procedures and international communication.
- [ ] are tested on first aid before they are allowed to take part in the training course.

i) Flight attendants have to be able to
- [ ] speak English and one more language.
- [ ] speak more than two languages.
- [ ] speak and write at least two languages.
- [x] speak and write at least German and English.

k) Before being invited to the training course, applicants
- [ ] only have to fill in the application form.
- [ ] fill in the application form and do a telephone interview.
- [x] fill in the application form, hand in the required documents and do a telephone interview.
- [ ] fill in the application form, hand in the required documents and do a language test.

3. Tips for your first day at work

https://www.first-day-at-work.co.uk

First of all, congratulations! You've landed a job – and hopefully the job that you were looking for. That means you've done everything right so far: you wrote an impressive letter of application, you were invited to the job interview, where you convinced the HR department that you were the right person for the job. Now it's your turn to prove them right.

If you've got time to spare, read the following tips that have been posted by people who have just found a job and have survived the first day at the new company. If you manage to follow some of the tips, your first day at work will be a piece of cake (well, not necessarily, but they will definitely help you get through the day without being a nervous wreck at the end of it …).

1. Do some background research

If you're not starting your new job tomorrow, you've still got enough time to do some background reading to prepare for the first day. I assure you that you'll be much more confident if you've got some facts and figures about the company at hand. By the way, I didn't read up on the company and asked some really stupid questions … *Lauren, 24*

2. Get a good night's sleep

You may find this tip unimportant or silly, but it isn't. The first day at a new job is very exhausting, because you meet a lot of new people who bombard you with lots of information. Do you think you will remember any of it if the only thing you want to do is go back to bed? *Trevor, 29*

3. Be on time

On your first day, you want to make a good impression. How do you think it will look if you arrive too late? So make sure you know your way to work, be it by car, bus, underground, bike or on foot. Ideally, test drive your route during rush hour – and then plan for some extra time, just in case. I know from personal experience that this is a good idea. I go to work by bus and had test driven my way to work before starting the new job, but hadn't calculated any extra time. On my first day, the bus I wanted to take was stuck in a traffic jam and I arrived 25 minutes late. I was totally stressed out and my new boss didn't seem happy at all. *Parker, 20*

4. Put some thought into your appearance

Do you remember what your future co-workers were wearing when you were at the office for the interview? Choose something that is appropriate (don't over- or underdress), but still something you feel comfortable in. Wear something that makes you look confident and professional. And decide what you want to wear a few days in advance, so that you could still go shopping if there was an emergency. In my opinion, this is extremely important. You know, I had been unemployed for a year and was extremely happy that I had finally found a job. However, I hadn't thought about the clothes issue beforehand, so on the morning of day one I found out that I didn't fit into my office clothes any more. Let me tell you, it's not a good feeling to be wearing something way too tight on your first day … *Isabella, 36*

5. Ask questions

Asking questions is the key to success – besides listening and taking notes. Pay close attention to what you are told, and don't hesitate to ask if you don't understand something straight away. So many things are new to you – it's completely normal that you need to clear things up. What I did is I secretly took notes on my colleagues' names, because I'm really bad at remembering them. I found out that my colleagues were much friendlier when I could address them by name. *Madeline, 22*

About us | Contact us | Copyright | Press | Cookies

Read the information found on a job centre website and answer the questions.

a) Who has posted the many tips on this website?   1 pt.

b) Why is it important to do some background research on the company before starting the new job?   1 pt.

c) Why is it very important to be fresh and clear on the first day at a new job?   1 pt.

d) What is Parker's advice?   1 pt.

e) What happened to Parker on his first day at work?   1 pt.

f) When should you decide what to wear on your first day at the new office?   1 pt.

g) Why was Isabella not feeling comfortable on her first day at work?   1 pt.

h) What did Madeline do to compensate for the fact that she is bad at remembering names?   1 pt.

The answer to the question below cannot be found directly in the text:

i) Why do people probably read this text?   2 pts.

C Use of Language

1. Mediation

Das Schuljahr hat gerade begonnen und Cameron, ein Austauschschüler aus England, der noch kaum Deutsch spricht, ist neu an deiner Schule. Dein Lehrer, Herr Waas, bittet dich, ihm beim Erklären einiger wichtiger Dinge, die an der Schule zu beachten sind, zu helfen. Vermittle jeweils für den Lehrer ins Englische [E] und für Cameron ins Deutsche [D].

LEHRER: Kannst du Cameron bitte sagen, dass er am Montag um 8.00 Uhr in der Schule sein soll und dann gleich zum Chemieraum gehen muss.

DU [E]: *On Monday you'll*

2 pts.

CAMERON: Yes thanks, I will, but where is the chemistry lab? And what's the teacher's name?

DU [D]:

2 pts.

LEHRER: Er hat bei Frau Müller Chemie. Vielleicht kannst du dich ja hier vor dem Lehrerzimmer mit ihm treffen und dann könnt ihr gemeinsam hingehen? Sag ihm bitte auch, dass das Kaugummikauen bei uns an der Schule verboten ist und wir es auch nicht dulden, dass Mützen im Unterricht getragen werden.

DU [E]:

4 pts.

CAMERON: All right, let's do that. Could you ask if I can use my smartphone in class? It has a dictionary and I don't understand much.

DU [D]:

2 pts.

LEHRER: Ja, Cameron darf sein Telefon dafür verwenden, aber auch nur dafür. Er braucht aber eine Sondergenehmigung vom Schulleiter, weil Handys bei uns ja sonst verboten sind. Und er muss bitte den Kollegen selbstständig deswegen Bescheid geben.

DU [E]:

_____ 4 pts.

CAMERON: All right, I will.

LEHRER: Sollte er noch weitere Fragen haben, kann er sich jederzeit an mich wenden. Vielen Dank, dass du weitergeholfen hast.

DU [E]:

1 pt.

2. Words and structures

Read the text, then tick (✓) the correct words. 10 pts.

I was on a trip to San Francisco. I was waiting ❶ the boarding announcement at Gate 35, ❷ I heard a voice on the public address system saying, "We apologise for the ❸ , but Flight 534 will now board from Gate 19". I picked up my luggage and carried it over to Gate 19. A few minutes later the same voice announced that Flight 534 would in fact be boarding from Gate 35. So, again, I gathered my carry-on luggage and ❹ to the original gate. Just as I arrived exhausted, the voice spoke again: "We would like to thank all passengers ❺ our physical fitness programme." ❻ , we boarded at Gate 35. A tall man put his hand luggage in the storage locker over my seat. Well, that must be the one who would be sitting next to me ❼ the flight. I was hoping that he was not the talkative type because I hate to talk to strangers during a flight. As we reached our cruising altitude he asked me, "Are you also flying to San Francisco?" I thought, " ❽ a stupid question," so I answered, "No, I'm booked on a flight to Paris." "Oh my God," the man said, "then you're on the wrong plane. This plane is flying to San Francisco." I looked horrified.

"Are you sure?" "Definitely." I tried to stay **_9_** and not to laugh out loud. I said, "I guess I'll have to ask the flight attendant for a parachute." Now the man looked horrified. "A parachute? What **_10_** do?" He then got the joke and didn't talk to me again until we reached San Francisco.

❶ ☐ by ☐ in ☐ to ☒ for	❷ ☐ which ☒ then ☐ when ☒ after	❸ ☒ inconvenience ☐ sorry ☐ accident ☐ attention
❹ ☐ walk back ☐ had gone ☐ was running ☒ returned	❺ ☒ for participating in ☐ participating with ☐ to participate in ☐ to take part	❻ ☐ On the end ☒ At the end ☐ Finally ☐ At least
❼ ☒ during ☐ while ☐ for ☐ through	❽ ☐ Not ☒ What ☐ Which ☐ So much	❾ ☒ calm ☐ in a calm way ☐ calmer ☐ calmly
❿ ☐ have you to ☒ are you going to ☐ you will ☐ you go to		

D Text Production

Choose one of the given topics. Write about 150 words.
Count your words and write the number at the end of the text.

25 pts.

What is the story behind the picture?

Write a story and include at least **four** of the following aspects:
- Who took the photo?
- Where was the photographer travelling?
- When was the photo taken?
- Why was the photographer allowed into the cockpit?
- What did the pilot explain?

© Tea/Dreamstime.com

or

School will be over soon – what now?

You are a reporter for your English school magazine. As you are planning to go abroad for one year after finishing school, you write an article about taking a gap year.

Write a text and include at least **four** of the following aspects:
- the reasons why you want to take a gap year,
- possible disadvantage(s) of taking a gap year,
- where you are planning to go,
- what you are planning to do,
- who you are planning to travel with.

Listening Comprehension – Transcripts

Hello, this is the listening exam. I am going to give you the instructions for the test. There are three parts to the listening exam. At the start of the listening texts you will hear this sound: ◀
You may write down your answers at any point during the listening exam.

Part One

In part one you will hear two news items. You will hear the texts twice. Before listening to the texts, you will have 20 seconds to read the tasks. You now have 20 seconds to read the tasks for item one.
You are now going to hear the first news item for the first time. After a short break, you will hear the news item again. ◀

News Item 1: The pardoning of the Thanksgiving turkey

Thanksgiving is one of the major holidays in the USA. Its origins can be traced back to the time of the Pilgrim Fathers, the first settlers to the newly founded colonies, who celebrated their first successful harvest. Today, it is a nationwide holiday, which is always celebrated on the fourth Thursday in November.
One rather peculiar tradition is the so-called pardoning of the turkey, when the US president saves one or more turkeys from being killed and eaten. There are different theories as to who started that custom. Harry Truman was the first president to be presented with a turkey as a gift to his family, but there are no records that he spared the bird. Some years later, John F. Kennedy freed one of the turkeys given to his family, but it was not an official pardon; it was rather a spontaneous action due to the massive size of the bird. Kennedy seemed to think that a turkey of 55 pounds was too big for his family to eat. The first time an official pardon was issued took place in 1987, when Ronald Reagan was asked whether he would pardon Oliver North, a man who was engaged in the so-called "Iran-Contra Affair", a political scandal during Reagan's presidency. As he did not want to answer the question, he preferred to pardon the turkey instead, in order to avoid further questions. Since George Bush senior's presidency two years later, the pardoning has been a permanent tradition.

You now have 20 seconds to read the tasks for news item two. You are now going to hear the second news item for the first time. After a short break, you will hear news item two again. ◀

News Item 2: What about a Batmobile?

Have you ever imagined being a superhero? What would driving a fantastic car like Batman feel like? This might be the line of thoughts that crossed 29-year-old Australian Zac Mihajlovic's mind a few years ago. And he didn't just stop at thinking. He spent two years of his life building an exact copy of the Batmobile shown in the first movie from 1989 in his backyard. It took Zac another year to work in all the details needed for a registered car licence. Now the car is not just a life-sized model – it is actually driving with licence plates, papers and all. The whole thing started with his grandfather, who told him that "any fantasy can become a reality", and he tried to prove that. But there is also a big problem he has with the car: Whenever he drives around, people regularly try to stop him to ask questions about the Batmobile or to take pictures of it. Once he even needed a police escort to get out of a place when he was in Sydney with the car. By the way, Zac doesn't fight criminals. He actually uses the car for charity work.

Part Two

> In part two you will hear an interview. Listen to some students talking about Halloween. You will hear the interview twice. Before listening to the interview, you will have 40 seconds to read the task. You now have 40 seconds to read the task.
>
> You are now going to hear the interview for the first time. After a short break, you will hear the interview again. ◄

Interview: What do you think about Halloween?

REPORTER: Hello everybody, this is Angelica Mitchell from Westport High School Radio. Today I'm reporting live from the classrooms. I want to find out how you guys celebrate Halloween, and what it is that you like best about this holiday. Oh, there is someone I know. Hi, Karen, what do you like about Halloween?

KAREN: Hi Angie. I like Halloween because it is a very special day for me. My older brothers, Chris and Michael, are married and have little children. But on Halloween they all come to our house and the whole family enjoys a nice evening together. That feels like in the old days, when they were at home all the time. I like that, and I'm looking forward to seeing them again on Halloween.

PETE: Hello, my name is Pete. What I like best about Halloween is playing trick or treat. You think that I'm probably too old for this? Maybe you're right. But my younger brother is only five, and I look after him when he walks around our neighbourhood. He usually gets a lot of sweets, and, afterwards, he shares with me. He always says this is my "payment" for helping him. That's funny!

KIRA: Hi, I'm Kira Parker. I like Halloween a lot. All those decorations and the lights create a special kind of atmosphere. It's like Christmas but with ghosts and witches. My parents cover everything in our house with spider webs and in every window there's a pumpkin with a candle in it. That looks amazing … and scary, too. Last year, my Dad even built a coffin with a mummy that could jump out when somebody touched it. Spooky!

ERIC: Hey everybody. My name is Eric Lancaster. Did you know that Halloween is an old special Celtic tradition? The people used to believe in ghosts that were allowed to come back from the dead. That was on the evening before the holiday of "All Saints" or "All Hallows", which is on November 1. Therefore the name: "All Hallows Eve". I think it's great that we still have this tradition. It is my favourite holiday.

TONY: Hi, I'm Tony. Halloween is my favourite holiday, too. I think it is the one where you can have the best food in the whole year. I love candy and on Halloween you can have tons of it. My mother usually bakes a big cake for the whole family and our family supper on Halloween is legendary. Forget about Thanksgiving, Christmas and Easter! Halloween tastes best!

DAVE: Hey, I'm Dave Bell. I'm sorry, but I don't like Halloween at all. Everyone is so excited about it! They spend so much money on candy, costumes and decorations. In my opinion, this is a waste of time and money. I don't like the noise and the lights everywhere, either. And I don't want to be tricked or scared all the time. That is really annoying.

MARY: Hello, my name is Mary, and I like Halloween a lot. I'm a big fan of costumes. Many people just wear something black or put a paper hat on. I like being creative with my costumes. Every year I come up with something new. It often takes weeks to finish my costume. Last year, I dressed up as a shark attack victim – and it was a big success. I'm almost finished with my costume for this year: a spider mutant.

REPORTER: Wow, that was a lot of information. Thank you all for your opinions. And "Happy Halloween"!

Part Three

> In part three you will hear a TV interview, conducted on May 22, 2014, between high school student Rachel Acorn and a TV reporter about an integrated prom. You will hear the interview twice. Before listening, you will have 30 seconds to read the task. You now have 30 seconds to read the task. You are now going to hear the interview for the first time. After a short break, you will hear the interview again. ◀

Interview: Integrated prom

1   REPORTER: Here is Cable 77 News, this is Zac McCain and I'm reporting from Rochelle, Georgia, a southern city in the US with about 1,400 inhabitants. Yesterday, for the first time
5   in decades, a school-sponsored prom was held at the local high school gym. You think that's nothing special? Well, let's ask Rachel Acorn, one of the participants. Hi, Rachel.
    RACHEL: Hello.
10 REPORTER: So, Rachel, can you tell us what was so special about your prom?
    RACHEL: Well, it was, as you have already said, the first school-organized prom in years. That means that before 2013 the students and their
15 parents had to organize the event on their own. However, these events were usually racially separated.
    REPORTER: Which means that there used to be a prom for black and one for white students?
20 RACHEL: That's true. And that did not change for a long period of time – for more than fifty years no one even questioned that habit.
    REPORTER: But something changed in 2013?
    RACHEL: Exactly. A couple of students didn't want
25 to celebrate separately. They wanted to spend this special evening with all of their friends.
    REPORTER: Tell us more about those students!
    RACHEL: Erm … I can't remember their exact names. Sorry. But there were two black and
30 two white girls, who were really close friends.
    REPORTER: What did they do?
    RACHEL: They came together and organized a private integrated prom – the first one ever to take place in this city.
35 REPORTER: Why had that never been done before?
    RACHEL: In the 1960s the first African Americans were allowed to enter high schools that used to be exclusively for white people in those days. When that happened here, the school
40 didn't want to organize a prom any more.
    REPORTER: And the reason was …?
    RACHEL: Actually, I don't know. But I think they might have been afraid of something bad to happen – a scandal or something like that.
45 REPORTER: And did anything bad happen at the first prom for black and white students?
    RACHEL: Well, the worst thing that happened was that younger students weren't allowed to show up because there would have been too
50 many people there. It was a great, peaceful party where people were enjoying themselves.
    REPORTER: So, I guess you appreciate what your colleagues did last year.
    RACHEL: Oh yes, of course. They are real heroes
55 to us because they showed the whole city – and the whole nation, too – that racial equality should be present in everyday life at all times. After their private integrated prom had been a success, the school couldn't ignore
60 that. I mean, we live in the 21st century! Equal rights should be protected and everyone must be treated in the same way.
    REPORTER: Indeed. So, Rachel, how was your own prom yesterday?
65 RACHEL: I had a great time. I guess all the others had one, too. Let's not forget that it was an event for young people who wanted to have some fun. No offence, but the media report about it as if it was something that should be
70 awarded with the Nobel Peace Prize. I believe black and white kids celebrating together should be perfectly normal and nothing special after all.
    REPORTER: No offence taken, Rachel. You are ab-
75 solutely right. Thank you for your opinion and your time. And good luck for the future.
    RACHEL: Thank you and you're welcome.

> You can now continue with the rest of the exam. Good luck!

A Listening Comprehension

Part One

*Listen to the news items and tick (✓) the right statements.
Only one answer per statement is correct.*

News Item 1: The pardoning of the Thanksgiving turkey   4 pts.

a) Thanksgiving is celebrated to remember the
- [ ] foundation of the new colonies.
- [X] arrival of the first settlers.
- [ ] Pilgrims' first harvest.

b) Harry Truman was the first president
- [ ] who spared a turkey on Thanksgiving.
- [X] who was given a turkey as a present.
- [ ] who officially celebrated Thanksgiving.

c) The first official pardon was issued by
- [ ] John F. Kennedy.
- [X] Ronald Reagan.
- [ ] George Bush senior.

d) Oliver North
- [ ] was indirectly responsible for the first turkey pardoning.
- [ ] wanted to become president instead of Reagan.
- [X] fought in the Iran War.

News Item 2: What about a Batmobile?   4 pts.

a) Zac Mihajlovic
- [ ] lives in Austria.
- [X] is 29 years old.
- [ ] was born in 1998.

b) He built his Batmobile
- [ ] with his grandfather.
- [ ] to fight crime.
- [X] in his backyard.

c) The car is so special because
- [ ] it has bullet-proof windows.
- [ ] even a police escort cannot stop it.
- [X] it has a real car licence.

d) Zac needed the police once because
- [X] there were people blocking his way.
- [ ] people took pictures of him in Sydney.
- [ ] they helped him fight some criminals.

Abschlussprüfung Englisch – Übungsaufgabe 2

Part Two

Interview: What do you think about Halloween?

*Listen to the interview. Some people are talking about Halloween.
Who thinks what? Write the correct letters in the chart.
Be careful: There is one more statement than you need.*

7 pts.

A I like Christmas more than Halloween.

B I don't have a great time on Halloween.

C My Halloween costumes are very special.

D Halloween brings the family together.

E My parents are very creative on Halloween.

F Eating is one of my favourite hobbies.

G I like being a big brother on Halloween.

H Halloween has a long history.

Karen	Pete	Kira	Eric	Tony	Dave	Mary

Part Three

Interview: Integrated prom

In part three you will hear an interview between Rachel Acorn and a TV reporter. You will hear the interview twice. Listen to the interview and fill in the missing information in the grid.

10 pts.

number of people living in Rochelle, Georgia	
where the prom took place the day before	
organizers of the prom before 2013	
period of time in which proms were racially separated	
reason why some students did not want to celebrate separately	
organizers of the integrated prom in 2013	
decade since when African Americans have been allowed at high schools	
reason why younger students were not allowed to go to the prom in 2013	
Rachel's reaction to her own prom	
Rachel's opinion about young black and white people celebrating together	

B Reading Comprehension

1. Theatre reviews

These people like to go to the theatre or they work there. Find the most suitable stage production (A–G) for every person (1–5).
Be careful – there are two more reviews than you will need.

5 pts.

❶ **Helen** (20) works in a bookshop. Her boyfriend invites her to a show based on songs by a group where an astrophysicist plays the guitar.

❷ **Diana** (21) goes to a show where a woman is turned into a bird by a sorcerer.

❸ **Susan** (20) is a member of the crew working on a famous show where actors and actresses dress up as animals.

❹ **Paul** (21) works at a theatre as a singer. He is actually in rehearsal for a show where he plays the role of someone whose father died in the war and who was left by his wife.

❺ **Leonie** (23) goes to a show where a main character is a disabled black man.

A   Swan Lake

Swan Lake is a ballet by Pyotr Ilyich Tchaikovsky, one of the greatest Russian composers. It was composed in 1875 and 1876 and had its premiere on March 4, 1877 at the Bolshoi Theatre in Moscow. The story is based on Russian folk tales and an old, German legend. It is about a princess called Odette, who is turned into a swan by an evil sorcerer's curse[1].

B   Porgy and Bess

Porgy and Bess is an opera based on DuBose Heyward's novel "Porgy". The music was composed by George Gershwin and contains lots of elements of spiritual, blues and jazz. The opera deals with African-American life in Catfish Row in Charleston, South Carolina, in the early 1930s. It tells the story of Porgy, a handicapped black man, who tries to rescue Bess from her violent and possessive lover Crown, and from a drug dealer called Sporting Life.

C   Snow White and the Seven Dwarfs

This Christmas holiday season, you should not miss "Snow White and the Seven Dwarfs – A Panto". A pantomime (or panto, as it is informally called) is a British tradition that goes back to the 17th century. It is always based on a well-known fairy-tale, but includes slapstick comedy, singing, dancing and cross-dressing. Most importantly, the audience is expected to participate. So if you and your family want to see Snow White hiding among the seven dwarfs in the forest and boo at the wicked stepmother, this adaptation of the fairy tale written by the Brothers Grimm is what you should go and see.

D The Wall

The Wall is a rock opera by Pink Floyd. It was presented as a double album and released in late 1979. It was performed live with theatrical effects and even made into a film. The main character in The Wall is "Pink". Pink struggles in life from an early age: he lost his father in the Second World War ("Another Brick in the Wall"), was abused by his teachers ("The Happiest Days of Our Lives"), had an overprotective mother and was abandoned by his wife later on. This leads to Pink's mental isolation from society – referred to as "The Wall".

E Kurios: Cabinet of Curiosities

The show "Kurios", which had its premiere in April 2014 in Montreal, is a production of the renowned "Cirque du Soleil". Like all the other very successful shows of the "Cirque", it contains spectacular acrobatic acts, and a lot of fantastic music and dance performances. The show features elements of "steampunk" and the story is set in the late 19th century, where a character called "The Seeker" invents a machine which can alter time and space – allowing him to meet beings from another dimension and to interact with them.

F We Will Rock You

"We Will Rock You" is a jukebox musical based on a big hit single of the same name and other songs by Queen. It was written by author Ben Elton in co-operation with Brian May and Roger Taylor. Brian May, Ph.D, is an astrophysicist, but is most widely known as the lead guitarist of Queen. The story of the musical is set 300 years in the future. Earth, called "Planet Mall", is controlled by the Globalsoft Corporation: all children listen to computer-generated music, wear the same clothes and hold the same thoughts and opinions. Music instruments are prohibited, and people are unfamiliar with rock music.

G The Lion King

Based on the 1994 Disney animated film, this musical tells the moving story of Simba, a lion cub, whose father is killed by his mean uncle. After living in exile, Simba returns to the kingdom now ruled by his uncle, revenges his father's death and becomes the new king. "The Lion King" is a worldwide success. It has been referred to as a "feast for the eyes and ears", because actors are dressed in colourful animal costumes and the catchy music was written by Elton John. Famous songs like "Can you feel the love tonight" or "Hakuna Matata" have the audience singing along. Suitable for the entire family.

person	❶	❷	❸	❹	❺
play					

1 sorcerer's curse = *Fluch eines Hexenmeisters/Zauberers*

2. The history of Halloween

The origin of our modern holiday "Halloween" goes back to the old Gaelic festival of "Samhain", which for the Celts marked the end of the harvest period and the beginning of the "dark season" of winter, and which was celebrated from sunset on October 31st to sunset on November 1st. It was the time when the cattle was brought back from its summer meadows and the preparation for the less fertile months began.

On Samhain, which was celebrated in what is now Ireland, the Isle of Man and parts of Scotland, the people lit bonfires and held special feasts and meals. There were also special offerings for the old gods and the "aos sí", which is a mystical and supernatural race comparable to fairies or elves, which the Celts commonly believed in. There was also the belief that on Samhain – as well as on Midsummer's Eve – the borders between this world and the world of the spirits could be crossed more easily, which made it possible for the dead to visit our world once again. However, this was not only a frightening event. The Celts believed that their ancestors wanted to join them on this date to make sure that they were well and protected. That is why people put empty chairs next to their own, which were meant for the dead members of the family.

Of course, not only the good and gentle spirits came to visit our world. Therefore, the Celts often wore special clothes and costumes to hide from the unpleasant and dangerous spirits. In those costumes they sometimes went from house to house and asked for blessings and small gifts. This tradition is still practised on Halloween by the many children that roam their neighbourhood playing "trick or treat". And just as the evil spirits that could do bad things to the people not welcoming the dead, the children play tricks on people who do not open the door or give them sweets.

Between the 4th and the 10th centuries, the Roman Catholic Church took over many pagan and Jewish holidays and shifted their own special days to dates of existing festivals and around them. The day of the birth of Christ, for example, became connected to the Roman "Festival of the Sun" and the "Passion" and "Resurrection of Christ" – now known as "Easter" – was linked to the Jewish "Passover". Thus, the practice and celebration of "All Saints' Day", also called "All Hallows' Day", where Christians should think about their dead saints, was shifted to the main date of Samhain – November 1st – turning the night before into "All Hallows' Evening".

Over the years, decades and centuries, the phrase was shortened to become the word "Halloween", which was still connected to the traditions and the belief of the Gaelic Samhain, where the spirits of the dead came to visit the living – just as the deeds of the Christian saints were commemorated on the day of "All Saints".

Today, however, many people do not remember the origin of traditions like going "trick or treating" or the carving of the pumpkins to look like evil spirits. They believe that it is just childish behaviour and has no purpose at all because the meaning behind those rites has been lost over the centuries.

Read the text and tick (✓) the correct box. 10 pts.

a) The Gaelic festival of Samhain is
- [ ] now a modern Christian holiday.
- [x] the origin of Halloween.
- [ ] the Celtic name for "harvest".
- [ ] still celebrated in the winter.

b) The celebration of Samhain took
- [x] about 24 hours.
- [ ] one night.
- [ ] two days.
- [ ] the whole season.

c) It was celebrated
- [ ] only in Scotland.
- [x] on all of the British islands.
- [ ] at least in Ireland.
- [ ] only in the UK.

d) The "aos sí" are
- [ ] gods of the Irish people.
- [ ] Celts that believed in elves.
- [x] some kind of fairies.
- [ ] Celts with superpowers.

e) The Celts believed that the spirits could come into our world
- [x] only on Midsummer's Eve.
- [ ] whenever they wanted.
- [ ] only on Halloween.
- [ ] only on Samhain.

f) Some chairs at the table were left empty on Samhain
- [x] because they were for the dead relatives.
- [ ] for the small gifts collected by the people.
- [ ] to turn unpleasant spirits away.
- [ ] only for good and gentle spirits.

g) If you do not open your door on Halloween,
- [ ] the children do not come to your house.
- [ ] evil spirits do bad things to you.
- [ ] you do not get sweets as a present.
- [x] some children may play tricks on you.

h) Christmas is linked to a
- [x] Jewish holiday.
- [ ] Roman festival.
- [ ] Gaelic celebration.
- [ ] Celtic tradition.

i) "Halloween" is
- [x] on October 31st.
- [ ] short for "All Hallows' Day".
- [ ] another name for "All Saints' Day".
- [ ] on November 1st.

k) People do not remember the meaning of Halloween because
- [ ] they do not want to be childish.
- [ ] it has no purpose at all.
- [ ] there are no real evil spirits.
- [x] the original meaning has been lost.

3. Slam

I'd never met anyone quite like Alicia's mum and dad before I started going out with Alicia, and at first I thought they were dead cool – I can even remember wishing that my mum and dad were like them. Alicia's dad is like fifty or something, and he listens to hip-hop. [...] He teaches literature at a college, and she teaches drama, when she's not being a councillor. Or she teaches people to teach drama, something like that. [...] They're all right, I suppose, Robert and Andrea, and they were really friendly at first. It's just that they think I'm stupid. They never say as much, and they try and treat me as if I'm not. But I can tell they do. I wouldn't mind, but I'm smarter than Alicia. [...] When we went to see films, she didn't understand them, and she never got what anyone was laughing at in *The Simpsons,* and I had to help her with her maths. Her mum and dad helped her with her English. They still thought she was going to go to college to do something or other, and all the model stuff was just her going through a rebellious phase. As far as they were concerned, she was a genius, and I was this nice dim kid she was hanging out with. [...]

At that family lunch, when I was invited because I was part of the family, I was just sitting there minding my own business when her dad asked me what I was going to do after my GCSEs[1].

'Not everybody is academic[2], Robert' said Alicia's mum quickly.

You see how it worked? She was trying to protect me, but what she was trying to protect me from was a question about whether I had any future at all. I mean, everyone does something after their GCSEs, don't they? Even if you sit at home watching daytime TV for the rest of your life, it's a future of sorts. But that was their attitude with me – don't mention the future, because I didn't have one. And then we all had to pretend that not having a future was OK. That's what Alicia's mum should have said. 'Not everybody has a future, Robert.'

'I know not everybody is academic. I was just asking him what he wanted to do,' said Robert.

'He's going to do art and design at college,' said Alicia.

'Oh,' said her dad. 'Good. Excellent.'

'You're good at art, are you, Sam?' her mum said.

'I'm all right. I'm just worried about if we have to do essays and stuff at college.'

'You're not so good at English?'

'Not at writing it, no. Or speaking it. I'm fine at all the rest.'

That was supposed to be a joke.

'It's just a matter of confidence[3],' said her mum. 'You haven't had the same advantages as a lot of people.'

I didn't know what to say to that. I have my own bedroom, a mum who's in work and who likes reading and who gets on my case if I haven't done my homework …

To be honest, I don't really know how many more advantages I could use. Even my dad not being around was a good thing; because he's not into education at all. I mean, he wouldn't actually stop me trying to study, but … Actually, maybe that's not true. It was always a thing between him and Mum. She was desperate to go[4] to

college, and he's a plumber[5], and he's always made decent money [...] As far as
people like Alicia's parents are concerned, you're a bad person if you don't read
and study, and as far as people like my dad are concerned, you're a bad person if you
do. It's all mad, isn't it? It's not reading and whatever that makes you good or bad.

From: Nick Hornby, Slam; London: Penguin 2017, S. 73–76

1 GCSE = General Certificate of Secondary Education *(entspricht in etwa dem Realschulabschluss)*
2 academic = *akademisch, d. h. sich weniger mit praktischen als mit geistigen Dingen befassend (z. B. in einem Studium)*
3 confidence = the feeling or belief that you are good at something
4 to be desperate to do sth = here: to really want to do sth
5 plumber = *Klempner/in*

Answer the questions.

a) What did Sam first think about Alicia's parents? 1 pt.

b) What is Robert's job? 1 pt.

c) Sam says that he is cleverer than Alicia. Name two reasons why. 2 pts.

d) What does Sam want to do after school? 2 pts.

e) Name one of the things we learn about Sam's mother. 1 pt.

f) What does Sam's dad think about education? 1 pt.

You cannot find the answers to the following questions directly in the text:

g) Why do Andrea and Robert think Sam is not very intelligent? 1 pt.

h) What does Sam mean when he says "It's not reading and whatever that makes you good or bad." (l. 47)? 1 pt.

C Use of Language

1. Mediation

Zusammen mit deinen Freunden kommst du auf einer Reise durch Schottland nach Glasgow. Als ihr in einem Hotel einchecken wollt, musst du für dich und deine Freunde die Fragen eines Hotelangestellten an der Rezeption beantworten. Dazu sprichst du dich während des Gesprächs mit deinen Freunden ab, die weitere Fragen haben. Übertrage die Informationen jeweils für deine Freunde ins Englische [E] und für den Angestellten ins Deutsche [D].

ANGESTELLTER:	Good afternoon, how can I help you?	
DU:	Good afternoon. We haven't made a reservation. Do you have any rooms for us anyway?	
ANGESTELLTER:	Yes, we do. How long would you like to stay?	
DU [D]:	**Wie lange** _____	1 pt.
FREUNDE:	Wollten wir nicht eine Woche bleiben und dann weiter an die Küste?	
DU [E]:	_____	1 pt.
ANGESTELLTER:	How many rooms do you need?	
DU [D]:	_____	1 pt.
FREUNDE:	Also, Laura und Christian wollen ein Doppelzimmer und Julian schläft sehr unruhig und hätte deswegen gern ein Einzelzimmer. Was ist mit dir und mir? Wir nehmen einfach ein Zimmer mit zwei Einzelbetten.	
DU [E]:	_____	2 pts.
ANGESTELLTER:	Would you like to have rooms with bathrooms or rooms with bathrooms in the hall?	
DU [D]:	_____	2 pts.
FREUNDE:	Das kommt auf den Preis an. Vielleicht kannst du mal fragen, wie viel die Zimmer kosten?	
DU [E]:	_____	1 pt.
ANGESTELLTER:	The single will be £39, the double or the twin room £72 a night. With the bathroom in the hall you would pay £15 less per room.	

Abschlussprüfung Englisch – Übungsaufgabe 2

DU [D]: _____ 3 pts.

FREUNDE: Dann nehmen wir die Zimmer mit Bad.

DU [E]: _____ 1 pt.

ANGESTELLTER: Excellent. Could you just fill out these forms for me, please?

DU [D]: _____ 1 pt.

ANGESTELLTER: Thank you. Here are your room keys. You can use the lift to get to the third floor. Enjoy your stay.

2. Words and structures

Read the text, then choose the correct words from the box to fill in the gaps. Be careful – there are more words than you need. Use each correct word only once. 12 pts.

| change • first • from • helped • major • meaning • off • on • opinion • over • popular • present • rich • story • taught |

In the (1) _____ "A Christmas Carol" by Charles Dickens, the reader is (2) _____ an important lesson. Ebenezer Scrooge, the main character, is a (3) _____ and nasty old man. He gets to see his past, (4) _____ and future with the help of three ghosts during the night before Christmas and finally realises that he has to (5) _____ his behaviour.

Charles Dickens called the story his "little Christmas book" and it was the novelist's (6) _____ of five Christmas books. "A Christmas Carol" was a great success right (7) _____ the beginning and (8) _____ six thousand copies were sold in one week. Originally written in _____ by Dickens, who was under financial pressure to pay (9) _____ a debt, the tale has become one of the most (10) _____ Christmas stories of all time.

Some historians have suggested that the popularity of the tale has actually played a (11) _____ role in shaping the (12) _____ of Christmas and the spirit of the holiday.

D Text Production

Choose one of the following tasks and write about 150 words.
Count your words and write the number at the end of the text.

25 pts.

Tell the story behind the picture.

Imagine you have taken this picture.

Write the story and include at least **four** of the following aspects:

- Where did you take the picture?
- Why did you take the picture?
- Were you on your own or was somebody with you?
- When did you see the mysterious white spot on the right-hand side of the picture?
- What do you think the white spot is? A ghost? Or only a reflection on the camera lens? Or …?

© Katzer/Philipp

or

Dear Diary …

Imagine you spent an awful holiday with your parents in an English-speaking country.
After returning home, you write a diary entry.

Write the text and include at least **four** of the following aspects:
- Where did you spend your holiday?
- What did you do?
- Where did you stay?
- What was so awful about the holiday? / What went wrong?
- What were you feeling or thinking?

Listening Comprehension – Transcripts

> Hello, this is the listening exam. I am going to give you the instructions for the test. There are three parts to the listening exam. At the start of the listening texts you will hear this sound: ◀
> You may write down your answers at any point during the listening exam.

Part One

> In part one you will hear two news items. You will hear the news items twice. Before listening to the texts, you will have 20 seconds to read the tasks. You now have 20 seconds to read the tasks for news item one.
> You are now going to hear the first news item for the first time. After a short break, you will hear the news item again. ◀

News Item 1: America returns into space

NASA's Orion space programme has finally begun. On Friday, 5 December, a rocket carrying the new spacecraft started off into the blue morning sky at Cape Canaveral, Florida – over 40 years after the last of the Apollo missions took American astronauts to the Moon and back. Actually, the launch had been planned to take place on Thursday, but NASA wanted to make sure everything went well. The new Orion spacecraft is able to get up to six people not only into the Earth's orbit, but is built to send them around the Moon in the 2020s and finally to Mars by the middle of the 2030s. Yet, this first successful flight test took place without astronauts, and the trip didn't last longer than four and a half hours. However, everything went perfectly fine as the spaceship was flying around the Earth two times. After the capsule had landed safely in the Pacific Ocean and was secured by US Navy ships, NASA mission control reported happily: "There's your new spacecraft, America."

> You now have 20 seconds to read the tasks for news item two.
> You are now going to hear the second news item for the first time. After a short break, you will hear news item two again. ◀

News Item 2: Italian nun wins "The Voice of Italy"

Shortly before the start of the blind auditions here in the UK, we've got some interesting facts on "The Voice" for you. Maybe you already know that the casting show was first aired in the Netherlands in 2010, but did you also know that it's a big success in lots of countries all over the world, such as Afghanistan, Australia, China, Indonesia, Brazil and Russia, to name but a few?
What I personally find interesting is the fact that in 2014, 25-year-old nun Cristina Scuccia won "The Voice of Italy" by singing Alicia Keys' love song "No One". At first it might seem strange when a nun sings lines like "You and me together through the days and nights, I don't worry 'cause everything's gonna be alright", but for Sister Cristina they were still ringing true: She said that without God and his help from above, she wouldn't have won the series. She also added that her reason for performing was to spread the message of God's love and not to earn money, an aim she thoroughly reached: Not only that "The Voice" regularly has audience shares of about 20% in Italy, Cristina's winning performance also earned her a record number of clicks on YouTube throughout the world.

Part Two

> In part two you will hear an interview. Reporter Marc White from CBC Radio 1 asks passers-by in downtown Vancouver how they usually spend their holidays. You will hear the interview twice. Before listening to the interview, you will have 40 seconds to read the task. You now have 40 seconds to read the task.
> You are now going to hear the interview for the first time. After a short break, you will hear the interview again. ◀

Interview: Five-star hotel or wilderness?

REPORTER: I'm Marc White from CBC Radio 1. We're doing a short survey on how people in Vancouver like to spend their holidays. Could you tell me your first name and say what you usually do when you're on holiday?

JOHN: I'm in a bit of a hurry, but that's an easy question to answer. My name's John and I'm 35. I've got a very stressful job, and I hardly ever go on holiday, but when I find the time, I only want to relax, so my wife and I usually go to a luxurious boutique hotel on Vancouver Island that doesn't allow small children. We go for long walks in the woods, get massages, go to the sauna and enjoy the fantastic food there.

OLIVIA: Hi, I'm Olivia and I'm a student at the University of British Columbia. I'm 21 and I love travelling, but I don't want to be seen as a tourist. Since I don't have much money, I usually go couchsurfing when I'm abroad. It's a great and cheap way to meet locals, make new friends and explore places far away from the typical tourist paths.

HAILEY: I'm Hailey and I'm 25 years old. I wouldn't like to go couchsurfing. I think it's dangerous to stay at the house of someone you don't know. I love travelling, but I don't earn much money, so I always stay at youth hostels. I always choose a small hostel so that there's a cosy atmosphere and travellers get in touch with each other easily.

CARTER: Hello, my name's Carter and I'm 16. In my summer vacation I usually go camping with my friends. I love hiking and fishing and being outside 24/7, so I wouldn't like to spend my holidays in any other way. My parents, in contrast, usually go on city trips together with their friends from the golf club.

JOSH: Camping is great, isn't it? I'm Josh and I'm 15. My parents bought a large mobile home five years ago, so we always go camping. I like sleeping in the comfy bed of the mobile home, whereas my younger brother always sleeps in a tent. We always go to the same campsite, which is great, because we meet the same people every year.

SARA: Hi, I'm Sara and I'm a mum. When we go on holiday, we usually rent an apartment at the coast. Staying at a hotel's just too expensive for a family of six and a dog, although I'd really love to not have to cook. We tried camping once, but it rained for a week, so that wasn't much fun.

LARA: My name's Lara and I'm from Germany. My family moved to BC three years ago. I've got some really nice friends here, but my best friend Lisa still lives in Frankfurt, so when I go on holiday, I always visit her.

REPORTER: Thanks everyone for sharing all this with me and our listeners. I hope you have a great time on your next holiday.

Part Three

> In part three you will hear an interview between Jennifer Brown and a TV reporter. You will hear the interview twice. Before listening to the interview, you will have 30 seconds to read the task. You now have 30 seconds to read the task.
>
> You are now going to hear the interview for the first time. After a short break, you will hear the interview again. ◀

An interview with Jennifer Brown

1 INTERVIEWER: Hi Jennifer. Thanks for taking the time to answer a few questions. Could you please tell our listeners about your childhood and how you became an actress and a writer?

5 JENNIFER: I'd love to. I was born in Vancouver in 1979. My parents are both Canadian, but my great-grandparents were from England and Germany. That's why I have connections to those two countries as well. After finishing
10 school, I worked in a hotel in San Francisco for five years, but that wasn't for me, so I decided to study for a degree in Science at the University of British Columbia. After two years, my scholarships ran out. I got into act-
15 ing as a way to pay for my tuition, but later I gave up my studies to work just as an actress. Now, I couldn't imagine doing anything else.

INTERVIEWER: What's it like working on the set? Can you describe your experience with the
20 other members of the cast?

JENNIFER: I don't think I can put into words how much fun we usually have on set. Everyone works really hard and they're totally supportive and respectful. I always feel like I can be
25 myself. It's great to be creative.

INTERVIEWER: With which famous actor or actress would you love to shoot a film one day?

JENNIFER: I'm sure it's a cliché, but Meryl Streep, or Jodie Foster. Jodie has always been my
30 idol.

INTERVIEWER: What role would you like to play some day? Any wishes?

JENNIFER: Well, maybe you think I'm crazy, but I'd like to play a main role in a Shakespeare
35 play. He uses wonderful words.

INTERVIEWER: Do people recognize you when you're out?

JENNIFER: A lot of people just stare, or tell me that I look familiar. And I get "Do I know you?" a
40 lot.

INTERVIEWER: Do you read the reviews of the movies you've made, you know, to see what people think about the character you're playing?

45 JENNIFER: I love to hear if people have enjoyed the characters I've worked on. My most important source of information are the online newspapers. I always read the reviews there, but I also use Facebook and Twitter to keep
50 up to date.

INTERVIEWER: What are your hobbies?

JENNIFER: Writing scripts, reading plays and training my two German Shepherds. I also love hiking and skiing, but I hardly ever find the
55 time.

INTERVIEWER: Do you speak any foreign languages?

JENNIFER: Not well enough to brag about. I can get by nicely with my French. All of the com-
60 mands I have for my dogs are in German.

INTERVIEWER: Have you ever been to Germany?

JENNIFER: Yes, I have, several times.

INTERVIEWER: What's the first thing that comes to your mind when you think of it?

65 JENNIFER: Fields and old castles, perfect little villages … I've been to Frankfurt and Munich, too, but I've never been to Berlin. I'd love to see the capital of Germany.

INTERVIEWER: Well, Jennifer, I'm so grateful that
70 you answered all my questions and I'm happy that we were able to get to know you better. Your fans and I wish you all the best for the future and hope to see you a lot on TV and on the big screen.

75 JENNIFER: Blessings and best wishes. Always!

> You can now continue with the rest of the exam. Good luck!

A Listening Comprehension

Part One

*Listen to the news items and tick (✓) the right sentence endings.
Only one sentence ending per statement is correct.*

News Item 1: America returns into space　　　　　　　　　　　　　　4 pts.

a) Orion's first flight took place
- [x] on December 5th.
- [ ] on a Friday in November.
- [ ] on a Thursday morning.

b) NASA's plan is to send people to Mars in
- [ ] the 2020s.
- [ ] 40 years.
- [x] the 2030s.

c) The flight test lasted for
- [ ] less than 4 hours.
- [x] 4 ½ hours.
- [ ] more than 4 ½ hours.

d) The capsule finally landed
- [ ] at Cape Canaveral.
- [x] in the sea.
- [ ] on a Navy ship.

News Item 2: Italian nun wins "The Voice of Italy"　　　　　　　　　　4 pts.

a) The casting show "The Voice" was originally
- [ ] British.
- [x] Dutch.
- [ ] Chinese.

b) In Italy,
- [ ] a 52-year-old nun won this year's series.
- [ ] Alicia Keys sang a love song in the final.
- [x] Sister Cristina performed the song "No One".

c) Cristina Scuccia's reason to participate in the casting show was
- [ ] to persuade others to become Christian.
- [ ] to earn money for her church.
- [x] to share God's love with the audience.

d) Cristina's performance reached
- [ ] mainly the Italian television viewers.
- [x] a worldwide audience.
- [ ] especially young people on YouTube.

Part Two

Interview: Five-star hotel or wilderness?

Listen to the interview. Some people are talking about how they usually spend their holidays. Who thinks what? Write the correct letters in the chart.
Be careful: There is one more statement than you need.

7 pts.

A We can't afford to stay at a hotel.

B I usually go on city trips.

C I don't want to be a tourist in the traditional sense. I want to meet local people and see their home town through their eyes.

D I always visit my best friend, who lives far away.

E Couchsurfing is too risky.

F I like camping, but I don't want to sleep on the forest floor.

G I love being outdoors.

H I want nature, silence and luxury.

John	Olivia	Hailey	Carter	Josh	Sara	Lara

Part Three

An interview with Jennifer Brown

In part three you will hear an interview between Jennifer Brown and a TV reporter. You will hear the interview twice. Listen to the interview and fill in the missing information in the grid.

10 pts.

the year Jennifer Brown was born	
nationalities of Jennifer's great-grandparents	
the period of time she worked in San Francisco	
the reason why Jennifer dropped out of university	
one reason why she enjoys working on set	
the reason why Jennifer likes Shakespeare plays	
how people react when they see Jennifer on the street (one aspect)	
her hobbies (two examples)	
a foreign language she speaks okay	
a German city Jennifer would like to visit	

B Reading Comprehension

1. Canada Facts and Figures

❶ Canada, whose name means "village" or "settlement", is the world's second-largest country after Russia. It consists of ten provinces and three territories. The country's smallest province is Prince Edward Island, named after Queen Victoria's father; the largest territory is Nunavut in the far north. There is the Pacific Ocean in the west, the Atlantic Ocean in the east and the Arctic Ocean in the north. In the South, Canada shares the world's longest land border with the USA. Four of the five Great Lakes are also part of the border between these two countries.

❷ Nunavut, which means "Our Land", is the coldest, largest and least populated territory. It is about the size of Western Europe, but only about 31,000 people live there, 85 % of whom are indigenous. It was created in 1999 and is therefore the youngest territory of Canada. Visitors can only fly into Nunavut as there are no roads that connect the 25 communities with each other or the rest of Canada. As rivers, lakes and the Arctic Ocean are frozen for three-quarters of the year, even very heavy vehicles can drive on the ice for more than six months. When the ice has melted, some communities can be visited by boat in July and August. In the summer months, the sun never sets, whereas in the winter, the sky is lit by the Northern Lights.

❸ There are two official languages in Canada – English and French – but that doesn't mean that every Canadian is bilingual. Quebec is the only Canadian province that uses French as its only official language. However, many people also speak English there, especially in Montreal and other popular tourist destinations.

❹ More than a century ago, in 1885, when people realized that it was necessary to protect plants and animals, the history of Canada's national parks started with the creation of Banff National Park in the province of Alberta in the Canadian Rockies. Today, Canada has got 39 national parks, which vary from between 9 km² and 45,000 km² in size. Some of the most popular activities are wildlife viewing, hiking, mountain biking, horseback riding, climbing, kayaking or canoeing, cross-country skiing, ice skating, skiing and snowboarding.

❺ One of the most famous tourist attractions is the Niagara Falls, located in the Canadian province of Ontario and New York State. The term "Niagara Falls" comprises three waterfalls, namely the Horseshoe Falls, the American Falls and the Bridal Veil Falls. One way to experience the falls is to go on a breathtaking "Journey Behind the Falls", taking an elevator down to the bottom of the falls and watching the water fall down from behind. Thrill-seeking visitors, however, might want to go on a cruise that travels past the American and Bridal Veil Falls to get as close to the Horseshoe Falls as possible. Although a lot more visitors tend to look at the falls on the Canadian side of the border, the American side is also worth a visit.

Find the five correct headings and match them to each paragraph (1–5). There are two more headings than you need.

5 pts.

A	All the Languages Spoken in Canada
B	How to Visit Niagara Falls
C	Geographical Facts and Background Information
D	Life in the Far North
E	Canada's Official Languages
F	Winter in Nunavut
G	National Parks in Canada

part of the text	❶	❷	❸	❹	❺
heading					

2. Vancouver, B.C.

Vancouver is a beautiful city with more than 630,000 inhabitants on the west coast of Canada, about 50 kilometres away from the border to the United States, but about 3,500 kilometres away from Ottawa, the capital of Canada. And it is definitely a rainy city. To be precise, it is the 9th rainiest place in Canada, and people say that if it rains in Canada, it rains in Vancouver. Vancouver is surrounded by water on three sides and is close to the Rocky Mountains. Its climate is one of the mildest in Canada. Vancouver is situated in the province of British Columbia, which is the third-largest province after Quebec and Ontario. The capital city of this province is not Vancouver but Victoria.

In 2010, the city of Vancouver hosted the Olympic and Paralympic Winter Games. Lots of people then visited the city for the Games, but Vancouver is still a popular tourist destination. Some of the must-sees are Christ Church Cathedral, Chinatown, Vancouver Art Gallery and the Capilano Suspension Bridge. Stanley Park, which is located on a peninsula in the heart of Vancouver, is one of the largest inner-city parks in North America and definitely worth a visit, with many attractions for the entire family on offer. Kitsilano, or "Kits", as the neighbourhood is usually called, is also popular among tourists. It is a fantastic destination if you want to do sports at Kits beach, eat out or go shopping. Many tourists also visit Gastown, the city's original settlement, to see the Gastown Steam Clock and to take a walk around the cobblestone streets.

Vancouver is a very clean city, much cleaner than most European or US cities, maybe because city authorities issue tickets for smoking, spitting or peeing in public places. What is more, Vancouver wants to become the greenest city in the world by 2020. That is why city authorities devised an action plan to reach this goal. One of the
25 aims, for example, is to make sure that every inhabitant lives within a five-minute walk of a park. They also want to plant 150,000 more trees and want to convince the inhabitants of Vancouver to walk and cycle more or use public transport.

The quality of life in Vancouver is said to be one of the best in the world. City authorities are proud to say that Vancouver is a "city for everyone". This is one of
30 the reasons why so many foreign people live in Vancouver. 52 % of the city's inhabitants do not speak English as their first language. However, 65 % of the inhabitants usually speak English at home. Although Vancouver is supposed to be a "city for everyone", housing is generally unaffordable, with Vancouver being the second most expensive housing market in the world.

35 Thirty years ago, the city's economy relied mainly on forestry, mining, fishing and agriculture. Today, tourism plays an important role, but industries such as the software development and film industries have to be mentioned in this respect as well.

Read the text and tick (✓) the right statement. 10 pts.

a) Vancouver
- [ ] is a city in Britain.
- [ ] is a city in North America.
- [✗] is located 50 miles away from the American border.
- [ ] has 630,000 inhabitants.

b) The Rocky Mountains are
- [✗] near Vancouver.
- [ ] a long way from Vancouver.
- [ ] in Vancouver.
- [ ] surrounded by water.

c) Vancouver
- [✗] is not the capital of British Columbia.
- [ ] is the capital city of British Columbia.
- [ ] is the capital of Quebec.
- [ ] is the capital of Ontario.

d) In 2010, Vancouver
- [x] had a record number of visitors.
- [ ] became the most popular tourist destination in Canada.
- [ ] was the rainiest place in Canada.
- [ ] organized the Olympic and Paralympic Games.

e) Stanley Park
- [ ] is the largest inner-city park in North America.
- [ ] has many attractions for children and adults alike.
- [x] is located close to Kitsilano.
- [ ] is located on the outskirts of Vancouver.

f) Gastown
- [ ] is great for doing sports.
- [ ] is fantastic for going shopping.
- [ ] is the birthplace of Vancouver.
- [ ] is famous for its clock powered by electricity.

g) Vancouver
- [ ] is the greenest city in the world.
- [ ] has got 150,000 trees.
- [ ] city authorities fine people for smoking in public.
- [ ] is the cleanest city in Canada.

h) In Vancouver,
- [ ] the public transport system is excellent.
- [ ] the quality of life is excellent.
- [ ] most people can afford to buy a house.
- [ ] most people walk or cycle to work.

i) _____ of the city's inhabitants speak English as their mother tongue.
- [ ] 35 %
- [ ] 48 %
- [ ] 52 %
- [ ] 65 %

k) _____ were very important for the economy of the city thirty years ago.
- [ ] The film industry and fishing
- [ ] Forestry and tourism
- [ ] Software development and agriculture
- [ ] Forestry and mining

3. An email from Vancouver

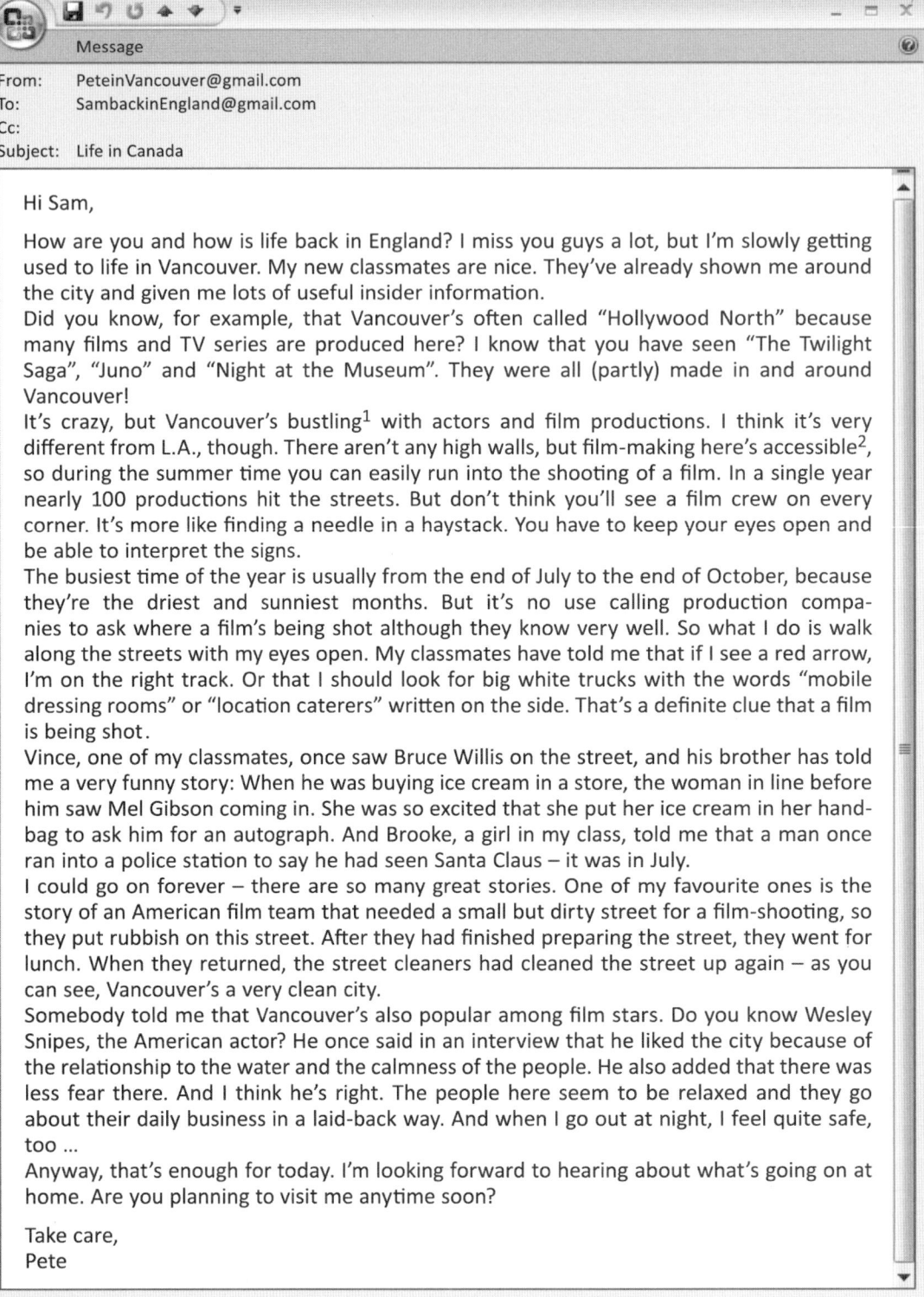

From: PeteinVancouver@gmail.com
To: SambackinEngland@gmail.com
Cc:
Subject: Life in Canada

Hi Sam,

How are you and how is life back in England? I miss you guys a lot, but I'm slowly getting used to life in Vancouver. My new classmates are nice. They've already shown me around the city and given me lots of useful insider information.

Did you know, for example, that Vancouver's often called "Hollywood North" because many films and TV series are produced here? I know that you have seen "The Twilight Saga", "Juno" and "Night at the Museum". They were all (partly) made in and around Vancouver!

It's crazy, but Vancouver's bustling[1] with actors and film productions. I think it's very different from L.A., though. There aren't any high walls, but film-making here's accessible[2], so during the summer time you can easily run into the shooting of a film. In a single year nearly 100 productions hit the streets. But don't think you'll see a film crew on every corner. It's more like finding a needle in a haystack. You have to keep your eyes open and be able to interpret the signs.

The busiest time of the year is usually from the end of July to the end of October, because they're the driest and sunniest months. But it's no use calling production companies to ask where a film's being shot although they know very well. So what I do is walk along the streets with my eyes open. My classmates have told me that if I see a red arrow, I'm on the right track. Or that I should look for big white trucks with the words "mobile dressing rooms" or "location caterers" written on the side. That's a definite clue that a film is being shot.

Vince, one of my classmates, once saw Bruce Willis on the street, and his brother has told me a very funny story: When he was buying ice cream in a store, the woman in line before him saw Mel Gibson coming in. She was so excited that she put her ice cream in her handbag to ask him for an autograph. And Brooke, a girl in my class, told me that a man once ran into a police station to say he had seen Santa Claus – it was in July.

I could go on forever – there are so many great stories. One of my favourite ones is the story of an American film team that needed a small but dirty street for a film-shooting, so they put rubbish on this street. After they had finished preparing the street, they went for lunch. When they returned, the street cleaners had cleaned the street up again – as you can see, Vancouver's a very clean city.

Somebody told me that Vancouver's also popular among film stars. Do you know Wesley Snipes, the American actor? He once said in an interview that he liked the city because of the relationship to the water and the calmness of the people. He also added that there was less fear there. And I think he's right. The people here seem to be relaxed and they go about their daily business in a laid-back way. And when I go out at night, I feel quite safe, too …

Anyway, that's enough for today. I'm looking forward to hearing about what's going on at home. Are you planning to visit me anytime soon?

Take care,
Pete

1 bustling = *geschäftig*
2 accessible = *zugänglich*

Read the email and then write down your answers.

a) What situation is Pete in at the moment? 1 pt.

b) Vancouver is also called Hollywood North: Name two films that were produced there. 2 pts.

c) In what way does Vancouver's film industry differ from America's? 1 pt.

d) How likely are you to see a film shooting? 1 pt.

e) What do you have to do to see one? 1 pt.

f) What did a customer do when Mel Gibson went into the ice cream store? 1 pt.

g) What did an American film crew do in one street? What happened? 2 pts.

h) What does Wesley Snipes think of Vancouver? Give one reason. 1 pt.

C Use of Language

1. Mediation

Du bist mit deinen Eltern im Urlaub in Kanada und ihr habt in der Lobby eures Hotels einen Flyer von „Vancouver's Breathtaking Tours" (siehe unten) gefunden. Deine Eltern verstehen aber nicht alles und bitten dich um Hilfe. Da dein Englisch besser ist als ihres, erklärst du ihnen, was auf dem Flyer steht.

Vancouver's Breathtaking Tours Ltd.

Totem Poles in Stanley Park

Capilano Suspension Bridge

Cliffwalk

Vancouver is a dynamic, multicultural city set in a spectacular natural environment. No matter what time of the year you visit, there are indoor and outdoor activities to please adults and children alike. Just ten minutes from the heart of downtown is Vancouver's oldest and most popular outdoor attraction – The Capilano Suspension[1] Bridge, located in North Vancouver.

Tour Description:
Our tours start in the heart of Vancouver. We have a few stops in the gorgeous Stanley Park on our way to the Capilano Suspension Bridge.
As Vancouver's oldest running attraction, the Capilano Suspension Bridge has been visited by many people for over a century. It is one of the longest, highest and most spectacular suspended footbridges in the world, spanning 137 metres across the Capilano River canyon at a height of 70 metres. Take a deep breath of fresh air and cross the gently swaying[2] bridge to the other side of the Capilano Canyon. While you are on the bridge, take a moment to admire the rare and amazing scenery surrounding you.
If you are not faint-hearted or scared of heights, you can also use the opportunity to enjoy the view of the rainforest from the Cliffwalk, the newest addition to the park opened in 2011.
We continue to visit the Capilano Salmon Hatchery[3], where you can watch salmon, and Cleveland Dam, where there's an impressive photo opportunity. Cleveland Dam blocks Capilano Lake and releases 100 million litres of drinking water each day!
The last stop of our tour is the top of Grouse Mountain (1,231 metres). We take a short 8-minute ride in the famous "Skyride" gondola to enjoy breathtaking views of the city, the ocean and the surrounding mountains.

Vancouver's Breathtaking Tours Ltd.
1155 Davie Street • Vancouver • Phone 0555-6846289

1 suspension bridge = *Hängebrücke*
2 to sway = *schwanken, schaukeln, schwingen*
3 salmon hatchery = *Zuchtanlage für Lachse*

Photos (from top to bottom): © Leszek Wrona / Dreamstime.com, © Katzer/Philipp, © Ronniechua / Dreamstime.com

Sage deinen Eltern in Stichpunkten,

a) wo die Capilano Suspension Bridge liegt. 1 pt.

b) wo der Tagesausflug beginnt. 1 pt.

c) wie lang die Hängebrücke ist und welche Höhe sie hat. 1 pt.

d) wann der Cliffwalk erbaut wurde. 1 pt.

e) welche Möglichkeit für die Besucher am Cleveland Dam besteht. 1 pt.

f) was man von der „Skyride"-Gondel aus sehen kann. 1 pt.

Deine Eltern möchten den Ausflug sehr gerne buchen, benötigen aber noch weitere Informationen, die nicht auf dem Flyer stehen. Sie bitten dich, an der Hotelrezeption nachzufragen. Übertrage ihre Fragen ins Englische.

Deine Eltern möchten gerne wissen,

g) ob die Tour täglich stattfindet. 1 pt.

h) um wie viel Uhr die Tour anfängt. 1 pt.

i) wie lange die Tour dauert. 1 pt.

k) ob es während der Tour auch einen Halt in Chinatown gibt. 1 pt

l) wie viel die Tour für Erwachsene kostet und ob es eine Schülerermäßigung gibt. 1 pt.

2. Words and structures

*Read the text, then choose the correct words from the box to fill in the gaps.
Be careful – there are more words than you need. Use each correct word only once.*   14 pts.

| after • as • beach • countryside • different • each • |
| has stopped • has taken • history • many • normal • others • |
| outside • took • visited • went • where • which |

For (1) _____ years now, history teacher Mary Green from Vancouver High School (2) _____ a group of high school students to Europe. (3) _____ year, it has been an adventure for both her and the students. The past spring was no different. They (4) _____ Scotland first, then drove through the English (5) _____ and crossed the English Channel to France to go to Paris. Each area was very (6) _____ from the others and each held its own charm.

In Scotland the group landed at Glasgow Airport and (7) _____ to Edinburgh immediately. After a short stay, they stopped briefly at Gretna Green, then drove into England, spent the night in Coventry and reached London the next morning. (8) _____ visiting London, they finally (9) _____ the Eurostar train to Paris, going underneath the English Channel. That was (10) _____ the trip ended. They left from Charles De Gaulle International Airport in the late afternoon on the tenth day.

Every place that they stopped at was a new adventure, (11) _____ was different for each person. Some loved Edinburgh best; (12) _____ preferred London. Most loved the (13) _____ of Paris. And they all learned this: to appreciate places (14) _____ Canada.

D Text Production

Choose one of the following tasks. Write about 150 words.
Count your words and write the number at the end of the text. 25 pts.

Applying for a job

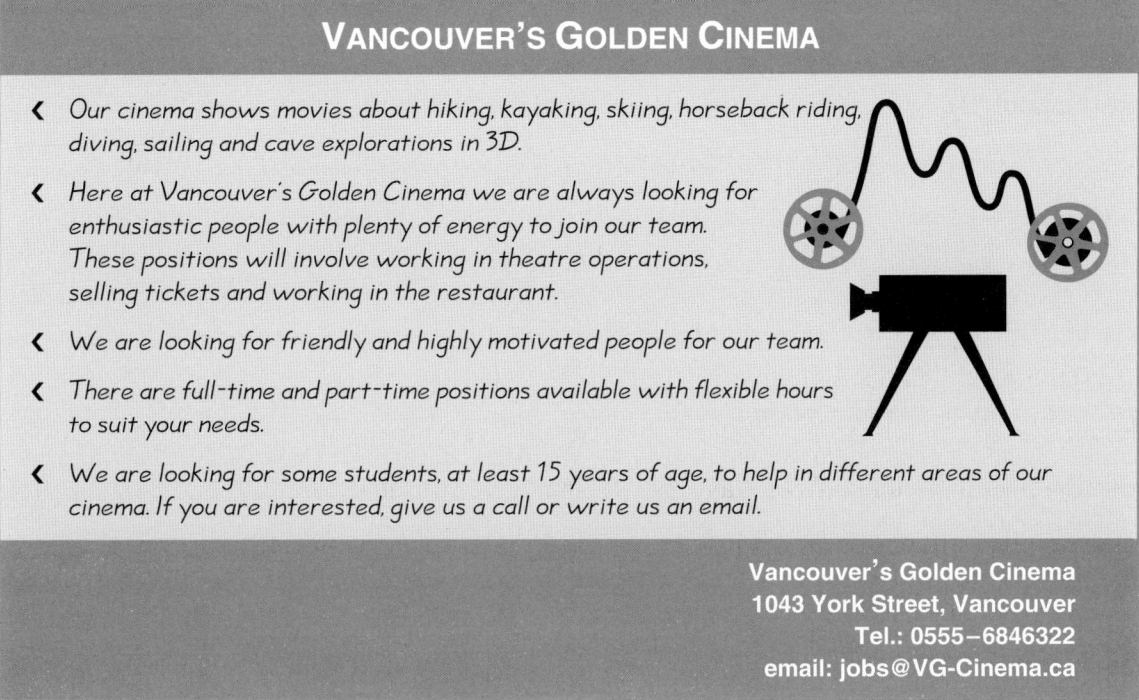

You decide to apply for the job. Write an email using a suitable **greeting and** a suitable **close**.

The following points should also be mentioned in your letter:
- Give three items of information about yourself.
- Say why you would like to work at Vancouver's Golden Cinema.
- Ask for more details of what students have to do.

___
or
___

Writing competition: "Your favourite film"

You want to take part in an English writing competition. Its title is "Your favourite film".

In your text, include what the film is about and three more aspects:
- Which actor(s) play the main role(s)?
- Where did you see the film?
- Why do you like the film?
- Who would you recommend this film to?

Hessen Realschule – Englisch
Übungsaufgabe 4

Listening Comprehension – Transcripts

Hello, this is the listening exam. I am going to give you the instructions for the test. There are three parts to the listening exam. At the start of the listening texts you will hear this sound: ◀
You may write down your answers at any point during the listening exam.

Part One

In part one you will hear two short listening texts. You will hear the texts twice. Before listening to the texts, you will have 20 seconds to read the tasks. You now have 20 seconds to read the tasks for announcement one.
You are now going to hear announcement one for the first time. After a short break, you will hear the announcement again. ◀

Announcement 1: Announcement on board

Good afternoon, ladies and gentlemen, and welcome on board Flight BA 7374 from London Heathrow to Singapore. My name is Zoe Anderson and I'm the purser of this flight. Our aircraft is under the command of Captain Jackson Moore and co-pilot Lily Davis, who has got her 500th flight today. Congratulations, Lily!
The time is now 2.30 p.m. Our flying time will be approximately 13 hours and 15 minutes. There is an eight-hour time difference between the UK and Singapore, so the time at your destination is currently 10.30 p.m. Our estimated time of arrival at Singapore Changi Airport is tomorrow at 11.45 a.m. local time. We will be travelling at an altitude of 11,000 metres at an airspeed of 600 miles per hour. You will be able to follow our route on one of the entertaining system channels. The weather in Singapore will be partly sunny with isolated showers. Temperatures during the day are expected to be around 30 degrees.
In a few moments, we will be coming round to offer you a choice of light meals and hot or cold drinks. Until then, sit back, relax and enjoy the flight …

You now have 20 seconds to read the tasks for announcement two. You are now going to hear the second announcement for the first time. After a short break, you will hear the announcement again. ◀

Announcement 2: Traffic update

It's Christmas Eve, my name is Leo Bell and this is BBC Radio 2 with a traffic update. I know that lots of our listeners are already on their way to visit their families for the holidays, but if you are planning to drive tomorrow, on 25th, and the day after tomorrow, on Boxing Day, in Southern England, make sure you check the weather forecast and road conditions before you hit the road. The Met Office has said that strong winds and heavy rainfall will develop later today and continue into the weekend. As a result of these weather conditions, the Highways Agency has issued a severe weather alert for all vehicles that may be at an increased risk of being blown over, such as motorbikes or high vehicles like caravans or buses. In addition, all motorists are advised to allow plenty of extra time if travel conditions are difficult or to think about delaying their journey, even if that means they can't celebrate with their loved ones.
Up-to-date information on road conditions is available at www.highways.gov.uk. For information on weather conditions, go to www.metoffice.gov.uk, listen to BBC Radio 2 or phone our hotline on 0300 244 6000.

Part Two

> In part two you will hear an interview. Listen to reporter Allison Hill of BBC London talking to passers-by in Oxford Street about nutrition. You will hear the interview twice. Before listening to the interview, you will have 40 seconds to read the task. You now have 40 seconds to read the task.
> You are now going to hear the interview for the first time. After a short break, you will hear the interview again. ◀

Interview: What's on your plate?

REPORTER: Hello. My name's Allison Hill of BBC London. I'm reporting live from busy Oxford Street on this rainy Saturday morning, where I'll be interviewing people about what is usually on their plates.
Excuse me, sir, do you have a minute? Could you give me your first name and tell me a bit about your eating habits?

HENRY: Of course. I'm Henry and I must admit that I'm a bit lazy when it comes to cooking. I'm single and I think it's too much work to cook just for myself, so I usually go to the pub with my colleagues after work. There's the "King's Head" next to the office and they usually have great specials.

REPORTER: And what's on your plate?

LIAM: Hi, I'm Liam and I'd love to be a good cook, but unfortunately I'm not. This means that my freezer's full of ready-made meals, which I simply pop into the microwave. At the weekend, I sometimes eat a fresh salad or some raw vegetables. However, my girlfriend gave me a cookery course as a Christmas present, so my cooking skills will hopefully improve …

CLARE: My name's Clare and I've been a vegan for two years. My diet is plant-based and I avoid all animal foods, such as meat, dairy products, honey and eggs. I also love Indian food, so I usually have a vegetarian curry for dinner. Vegan food is not as boring as many people think.

FINN: Vegan food? Not for me, thank you! There's nothing I enjoy more than a big chunk of steak. All my family love meat, no matter what: pork, beef, veal, lamb, chicken – I could go on forever. We also like to try exotic types, such as crocodile. In the summer, we have a barbecue at least once a week. I'm Finn by the way.

COLIN: You should really consider your health, Finn! I'm Colin and I'm a vegetarian. Since I don't have a garden of my own and can't afford to buy organic food all the time, I got involved in a community garden last year. We share a garden and grow all kinds of fruit and vegetables, which is great fun and really rewarding.

HANNA: My name's Hanna. What a great idea to join a community garden – I moved to London two months ago and I find it very difficult to make friends. I bet being part of a project like this would help me meet nice people who are on the same wavelength. I consider myself a "part-time vegetarian", because I usually eat vegetarian meals, but when I go out for dinner, I sometimes order fish or chicken.

TESSA: Hi there, I'm Tessa. One of my new year resolutions is to lose some weight. That's why I'm trying to cut down on sugar and carbohydrates. I recently read an article about animal transports, so I decided not to eat any more meat for ethical reasons.

REPORTER: Thanks everyone for sharing all this with me and our listeners. I hope you have a great time on your next holiday.

Part Three

> In part three you will hear an interview between Amy Smith, the world-famous Australian singer, and a radio reporter. You will hear the interview twice. Before listening to the text, you will have 30 seconds to read the task. You now have 30 seconds to read the task.
>
> You are now going to hear the interview for the first time. After a short break, you will hear the interview again. ◂

An interview with Amy Smith

INTERVIEWER: It's two minutes to two on this beautiful Tuesday afternoon. This is BBC Radio 2 with a special broadcast. Today we are talking to Amy Smith. She is now with us live from Sydney. Good afternoon, Amy.

AMY: Hello everyone.

INTERVIEWER: Amy, you have fans throughout the world. Your latest album "My soul, my life" is high up in the charts in 31 countries and has sold over 150,000 copies in the UK alone. How do you do it?

AMY: Well, I try to be myself. When I sing a song, I tell authentic stories – stories that many teenagers can relate to, such as feeling lonely, angry or insecure. I sing about heartbreak, being bullied or moving to a new city. I strongly believe that clichés about love are not what people want to hear these days. Of course, without my fans, my huge success wouldn't have been possible.

INTERVIEWER: I see. So are the stories you tell in your songs true?

AMY: Yes, most of them are. Although I have to admit that I do make the odd change to make them more interesting to listen to. But all my songs are authentic and sung with passion.

INTERVIEWER: Well, that certainly explains why all your concerts across Europe have already sold out and there's a long waiting list for your tickets.

AMY: I'm really flattered. There'll be six concerts in Europe's capitals: London, Paris, Madrid, Berlin, Vienna and Rome.

INTERVIEWER: Vienna is a special city for you, isn't it?

AMY: Yes, you're right. My fiancé is from Vienna, which is why I'll be staying there for two weeks this summer. I love the city. It's very romantic.

INTERVIEWER: I'm sure it is! So can we expect a wedding soon?

AMY: Yes, after my tour in August, but I'm not going to tell you any more details, so please don't ask!

INTERVIEWER: How important is family to you? I mean, I assume you must travel an awful lot because of your job. How do you keep the balance between your job and your family?

AMY: My family's my greatest priority, though I do love my job. Although it's sometimes hard to keep the balance between my job and my family, we manage quite well, I think. My fiancé usually accompanies me on my trips, so I get to see him quite a lot. I'm very lucky that he's prepared to travel with me, because it means that he had to give up his job.

INTERVIEWER: Can I ask you how you managed to become this famous? I know teenage girls throughout the world are aching to find out.

AMY *(laughs)*: Well, I don't know to be honest. There's certainly no such thing as a universal formula or a set of rules which you need to follow. I guess I was just extremely lucky and I've always loved singing and writing songs. When I was at school, I used to sing in the school choir and I was the lead singer of our school band. We gave concerts at our school, and did gigs in our area, such as weddings and large birthday parties. And then, one day, I received a phone call, which was totally unexpected, and a man asked me whether I wanted to sign a contract for my current record company. I was literally jumping for joy. That's essentially where it all started ...

INTERVIEWER: Well, Amy, I know you're very rushed since you have a plane to catch. Thank you so much for your time. Enjoy Europe and all the best to you.

AMY: It's been my pleasure.

> You can now continue with the rest of the exam. Good luck!

A Listening Comprehension

 Part One

Listen to the announcements and tick (✓) the right statements. Only one answer per statement is correct.

Announcement 1: Announcement on board 4 pts.

a) The announcement was made
- [ ] on board Flight PA 7374.
- [ ] on a flight to London Heathrow.
- [ ] on board Flight BA 7374.

b) The person speaking is
- [ ] the purser.
- [ ] the co-pilot.
- [ ] the pilot.

c) The plane will land in Singapore at about
- [ ] 11.45 a.m.
- [ ] 10.30 p.m.
- [ ] 2.30 p.m.

d) There will be … in Singapore.
- [ ] clear skies
- [ ] a lot of heavy rain
- [ ] sun and rain

Announcement 2: Traffic update 4 pts.

a) The announcement was made on
- [ ] December 24th.
- [ ] December 25th.
- [ ] December 26th.

b) There will be difficult road conditions
- [ ] in the South of England.
- [ ] on Boxing Day only.
- [ ] according to the Met Office.

c) All road users
- [ ] are in danger of being blown over.
- [ ] have to expect longer travel times.
- [ ] should travel by caravan or bus.

d) It is possible to get details on weather conditions by
- [ ] calling the BBC hotline.
- [ ] going to the website of the Highways Agency.
- [ ] turning on the TV.

Part Two

Interview: What's on your plate?

Listen to the interview. Some people are talking about their eating habits. Who thinks what? Write the correct letters in the chart.
Be careful: There is one more statement than you need.

7 pts.

A I don't eat any animal products at all.

B I want to eat fewer sweets.

C Cooking for me means heating up what's in the freezer.

D Cooking is too much work for one person.

E I grow my own fruit and vegetables.

F I'm a meat eater and I love barbecues.

G I always eat out at expensive restaurants.

H I'm not a strict vegetarian.

Henry	Liam	Clare	Finn	Colin	Hanna	Tessa

Part Three

An interview with Amy Smith

In part three you will hear an interview between the singer Amy Smith and a radio reporter. You will hear the interview twice. Listen to the interview and fill in the missing information in the grid.

10 pts.

the day the interview takes place	
the country Amy is in when doing the interview	
number of countries where Amy's album is in the charts	
number of copies of "My soul, my life" sold in the UK	
one topic Amy sings about	
number of cities in Europe where concerts will take place	
Amy's plans after her European tour	
reason why Amy's fiancé is able to travel with her	
where Amy sang with the school band (one example)	
reason why Amy is in a hurry	

B Reading Comprehension

1. Book reviews

The following people are all looking for a book to buy. Find the most suitable book for every customer (1–5) and write down the correct letter (A–G) in the table below. Be careful – there are two more books than you will need.

5 pts.

❶ **John** (21) studies law at university. In his free time he likes to read books about history, 16th century history in particular.

❷ **Julia** (19) does general administrative work in an office – a stressful job. She enjoys reading short stories a lot, especially because she only has time to read whilst travelling to work by bus in the mornings.

❸ **Ryan** (20) works as a tourist guide. He is therefore very interested in travelling and visiting places. He has been dreaming about visiting the west coast of the United States.

❹ **Kate** (22) is a professional swimmer. In her leisure time she reads non-fictional literature, such as books about the most exotic animals. She also likes photography.

❺ **Anthony** (20) is a bus driver in central London. Due to his busy job he seeks relaxation in detective stories. Anthony does not have a lot of time to spare.

A   The Golden Guide to New York

This new edition of "The Golden Guide" series is truly revolutionary in layout and is a must-read for the serious tourist or people who work in the industry. Numerous insider tips recommend the best restaurants, and the fanciest bars and clubs, whilst also providing factual information usually found in traditional guide books. Your visit to New York will be very special indeed if you use this book as your companion.

B   Finding Nemo – The True Story?

Are you interested in the sea? Would you like to find out more about the most exotic fish around? If your answer is "yes" to both questions, then this book about the hidden secrets of the sea is most certainly the right choice for you. With its many photographs as well as serious comments and facts, "Finding Nemo – The True Story" will take you on a journey to the bottom of the sea.

C Henry VIII and the Tudor Realm

This 400-page volume deals with every aspect of sixteenth-century Tudor England, including the most private affairs of King Henry VIII and his legacy to his successors. As such, it offers a substantial account in great detail of life under the Tudors, including the notorious religious politics of the period. A must-read for anyone interested in history.

D David Patterson's

Yet another set of ordinary short stories? – No! Although "David Patterson's" consists of twenty-four short stories, they are by no means ordinary, and are very exciting. Whilst they are based on true events, the author's ironic humour is reflected in the stories. A perfect fit for anyone short of time and in need of a rest in today's stressful world.

E Parrot and Cat

This new edition of the world-famous tale "Parrot and Cat" is a completely invented, yet humorous account of two animals going on holiday together. It is a ten-page booklet and, as such, fits perfectly into your coat pocket. Read it during your five-minute coffee break and feel good!

F The Natural Beauties of San Francisco

Discover San Francisco and its natural beauties today! This book is full of high-quality pictures and photographs portraying the city of San Francisco and its sights, but also the city's natural attractions, including major parks. This is your chance to discover the city's hidden attractions. Anyone who picks this book up will never want to put it down! It is undoubtedly the cheapest and quickest way of relaxing, as it is just like a short holiday!

G The Secret Adventures of Sherlock Holmes

Another collection of long, insipid stories? – No way! This collection is exactly the opposite! Thirty-two short adventures, each consisting of about ten pages, comprise this truly revolutionary style of Sherlock Holmes' secret adventures. The cases of this famous detective have been carefully reviewed and adapted to the twenty-first century. Enjoy!

customer	❶	❷	❸	❹	❺
book					

2. School life abroad

This week "Teens First Magazine" contains a special article about Tanja Huber. She is an ordinary fifteen-year-old girl from Fulda, Germany, who has been staying with a host family and going to an English school for the past few months. Our reporter Joe Thompson met her for the interview.

When I met Tanja for the first time, I was impressed by her English. "During the first month in which I did a language course in London and my four months here in Bristol I've learned a lot," Tanja says. "But when I first came here, I had a lot of problems. I couldn't understand what people were saying, because I simply didn't know enough words." "My English was rubbish," she adds with a laugh and explains that this was one of the reasons why she decided to spend an entire school year in an English-speaking country. "I'm really happy that I've got another seven months to go."

Tanja says that she gets along with her host family really well and that she has become close friends with the two twin daughters, who are fourteen years old. Tanja enjoys living with two "sisters", as her own brother, who moved out three years ago, is seven years older than she is. Tanja goes to St Thomas College in Bristol. Although school is very different in England, Tanja has got used to it, and she says that she enjoys it a lot. Wearing a school uniform is one of the things she did not like at first, but that has changed. What she likes about it is that she does not have to think about what to wear to school every morning. "It saves a lot of time," she says. "I have to wear a blue skirt and blazer or pullover with the school's coat of arms[1] and a white polo shirt. I especially like it that we are allowed to wear a polo shirt instead of a blouse, because it is much more comfortable. I also like the colour of the uniform – it's my favourite one apart from green."

Registration is another thing that was new to her. Every morning and every afternoon after lunch pupils have to go and register to show that they are in school. There is a quick registration in every lesson, too. Teachers call out the pupils' names, and pupils have to shout out, "Yes, Sir" or "Yes, Madam". If a pupil is not there, everyone knows immediately, and it is very hard to miss a class on purpose.

As school starts at 9 o'clock, Tanja is happy that she can sleep late even on school days (compared to Germany), because St Thomas College is just a five-minute bike ride away from home. So she sleeps until quarter past eight, has a quick shower and some fruit and cereal or a slice of toast and a cup of tea for breakfast before leaving the house with her "sisters" at quarter to nine. At the weekends, however, her host family sometimes prepare the traditional "full English breakfast" with bacon, sausages, baked beans, a fried egg and a grilled tomato. It was new to her that this hot breakfast is also called "a fry-up". She says that she is glad that the full English breakfast is reserved for special occasions, though, because she prefers a healthier start to the day.

40 Although Tanja misses her parents very much, she has got so used to life in England that she wants to train with an English company after passing her GCSEs[2] back in Germany and taking a gap year in Australia.

1 coat of arms = *Wappen*
2 GCSE = General Certificate of Secondary Education *(entspricht dem Realschulabschluss)*

Read the magazine article and tick (✓) the right statements. 10 pts.

a) Tanja Huber
- ☐ was interviewed by a fifteen-year old girl.
- ☐ is from Germany.
- ☐ moved to England with her family.
- ☐ had a lot of problems at home.

b) Tanja's English
- ☐ is excellent.
- ☐ is not good.
- ☐ is average.
- ☐ could be better.

c) At the time of the interview, Tanja had already been in England for
- ☐ one month.
- ☐ four months.
- ☐ five months.
- ☐ seven months.

d) Tanja's brother is
- ☐ three years old.
- ☐ seven years old.
- ☐ fourteen years old.
- ☐ twenty-two years old.

e) The school uniform Tanja has to wear
- ☐ is green.
- ☐ is her least favourite colour.
- ☐ is white and blue.
- ☐ consists of a skirt and a blouse.

f) Registration
- ☐ is a type of training.
- ☐ is a way of finding out whether every pupil is in school.
- ☐ is a school uniform with the school's coat of arms.
- ☐ only takes place in the mornings.

g) Tanja goes to school
- ☐ by bike.
- ☐ without having had breakfast.
- ☐ after eating a full English breakfast.
- ☐ on her own.

h) On school days, Tanja leaves the house
- ☐ at 8.15 a.m.
- ☐ at 8.45 a.m.
- ☐ at 9 p.m.
- ☐ at 8.45 p.m.

i) The traditional English breakfast
- ☐ includes baked beans and fruit.
- ☐ includes bacon and cereal.
- ☐ is a healthy meal.
- ☐ is also called "a fry-up".

k) After her GCSEs and some time abroad, Tanja will
- ☐ stay in Germany.
- ☐ train with a company in Australia.
- ☐ go back to Bristol.
- ☐ go back to England.

3. An Unforgettable Trip to London

Dear Diary,

This has been the best birthday present ever! My mum wanted my 18th birthday to be really special. As we live in a small flat, I couldn't have a big party, so my mum had saved up and had bought plane tickets for me and herself to London. When I woke up on my birthday, the tickets were sitting on the breakfast table. I couldn't believe my eyes – what a great surprise!

In the evening, we took the last flight to Gatwick Airport. As it was really late when we arrived at our hotel in the city centre, we had something to drink at the hotel bar and went straight to bed, because we wanted to be really fit for the next day.

After eating a full English breakfast, we left the hotel. We walked along the Thames up to the Houses of Parliament, heard Big Ben chime and went on the first ride of the London Eye that day when it opened at 10 o'clock. We were in capsule 18, which was quite a coincidence considering I had just turned 18. I didn't want to go on a traditional sightseeing tour, so we went on a city cruise instead. Seeing London from the water was special. We got off at Tower Pier and visited the Tower, which was very interesting.

We decided that we had done enough sightseeing for the day. After having had a light lunch, we wanted to do some serious shopping, so we took the Tube to Knightsbridge. My mum insisted on going to Harrods, because she had always wanted to see the famous Food Halls. At first, I didn't want to go, but once inside, I was really impressed. We then went on to browse the women's clothing. When I looked around, I suddenly saw an attractive brown-haired woman who looked just like Kate – I mean Catherine, the Duchess of Cambridge. I was really excited and turned around to tell Mum, but when I looked again, the woman had disappeared. Still, I'm sure it was her!

Our hotel was close to Leicester Square. We were on our way back to the hotel, when we noticed a large crowd in front of one of the cinemas. We stopped to find out what was going on – lots of reporters, photographers and camera teams were standing at a red carpet. We asked a policeman and he explained that it was the premiere of "The Second Best Exotic Marigold Hotel". Fans were waiting for Judi Dench, Richard Gere, Bill Nighy and other members of the cast to appear. My mum suddenly got all excited; she checked her appearance and tried to get as close to the red carpet as possible. She is Richard Gere's biggest fan and was hoping to get an autograph. It was funny: I had the feeling that we had just switched roles. Suddenly I was the mother and she was an eighteen-year-old girl. Although our feet were killing us, my mum made us wait for the stars to appear – and it was worth it. She got her autograph and Dev Patel, the really cute protagonist of the film (I had seen him in "Slumdog Millionaire") smiled at me. Wow.

I'm about to fall asleep now. I'll write more about the trip tomorrow.

Read the diary entry and then answer the questions in complete sentences.

a) Why wasn't the girl allowed to celebrate her birthday at home? — 1 pt.

b) What was her mother's birthday surprise? — 1 pt.

c) What did they do when they arrived at their hotel? — 1 pt.

d) Which famous sights did they see on the next day? (Name two sights.) — 1 pt.

e) Which means of transportation did they use during the day? — 1 pt.

f) Which department store did they go into? — 1 pt.

g) Who did the girl think she saw there? — 1 pt.

h) What did they see on their way to the hotel? — 1 pt.

The answer to the question below cannot be found directly in the text:

i) Why did the girl write that she and her mother had switched roles? — 2 pts.

C Use of Language

1. Mediation

Dein kleiner Bruder muss im Fach Geographie ein Referat über eine Sehenswürdigkeit in London halten. Er hat bereits eine Internetseite zum „London Eye" gefunden und bittet dich jetzt, ihm zu helfen, da du besser Englisch sprichst. Er hat dir Fragen aufgeschrieben, die du ihm auf Deutsch beantworten sollst.

The London Eye

The London Eye Building

Riverside Building, County Hall, Westminster Bridge Road, London SE1 7PB

Tickets & Prices

We offer more than fifty different types of tickets.
Click here for information on our Fast Track and Flexi Tickets.

Standard Ticket

(30 minutes flight time)
- Adults £21.50
- Seniors (60 and over with valid ID) £18.50
- Children (4–15 years with valid ID) £15.50
- Children (under 4 years with valid ID) Free
- Family of Four (2 adults 16+, 2 children under the age of 16) £74

To buy a ticket, go to our ticket office, call our booking line on +44(0)871 781 3000 or visit www.londoneye.com. If you pre-book your tickets online at least 24 hours in advance, you will receive a discount of up to 20%.

Opening Times

Click for more information:
Jan – Feb – Mar – Apr – May – June – July – **Aug** – Sept – Oct – Nov – Dec
- Monday, Tuesday, Wednesday, Thursday, Saturday, Sunday: 10 a.m. – 9.30 p.m.
- Friday: 10 a.m. – 11.30 p.m.

Getting to the London Eye

Situated on the South Bank of the River Thames, just opposite the Houses of Parliament, the London Eye is easy to get to:
- Underground: You can easily walk to the London Eye from several London Underground stations: Waterloo (nearest Underground station), Embankment, Charing Cross and Westminster. It is a short five-minute walk from Waterloo Station.
- Bus: 211, 77 and 381. Most London sightseeing bus tours include the London Eye.

About us | Contact us | Copyright | Press | Cookies | Accessibility

adapted from www.londoneye.com

Abschlussprüfung Englisch – Übungsaufgabe 4

Beantworte die Fragen in Stichpunkten.

a) Wie lange dauert eine Fahrt im London Eye? — 1 pt.

b) Wie viel kostet die Eintrittskarte für einen Teenager? — 2 pts.

c) Was muss man vorlegen, um ermäßigte Tickets zu bekommen? — 1 pt.

d) Wo kann man Tickets kaufen? — 1 pt.

e) Mit welchen öffentlichen Verkehrsmitteln ist das London Eye zu erreichen? (2 Informationen) — 1 pt.

Dein Bruder möchte gerne eine Mail an die Betreiber der Homepage schreiben, um weitere Informationen für sein Referat zu erfragen. Hilf ihm erneut, indem du seine Fragen bzw. Anregungen auf Englisch formulierst.

f) Er möchte wissen, ob man eine Filmkamera mit ins London Eye nehmen darf. — 1 pt.

g) Ihn interessiert, ob vielen Leuten schlecht wird, wenn sie damit fahren. — 1 pt.

h) Er fragt sich, welche Prominenten schon mit dem London Eye gefahren sind. — 1 pt.

i) Er würde gerne wissen, ob es Filme gibt, in denen das London Eye zu sehen ist. — 2 pts.

k) Er findet es schade, dass es diese Internetseite nur in englischer Sprache gibt. Die Informationen sollten auch in anderen Sprachen angeboten werden. 2 pts.

_____

_____

l) Er möchte sich bedanken, dass sie sich die Zeit nehmen, ihm zu antworten. 1 pt.

_____

2. Words and structures

Read the text, then tick (✓) the correct words. 11 pts.

Infrasound is sound that is ❶ to be detected ❷ the human ear. It is ❸ believed that the first observation of naturally-occurring infrasound was after the Krakatoa volcanic eruption in 1883. One of the pioneers ❹ modern infrasonic research was the French scientist Vladimir Gavreau, born in Russia as Vladimir Gavronsky. He ❺ interested in infrasonic waves during an ❻ in his lab in the 1960s ❼ he and his assistant experienced pain in the ear although no audible sound could be detected by his microphones. However, some animals are able to recognize infrasonic waves that natural disasters ❽ cause, and elephants ❾ to hear infrasound from two and a half miles away. In 2003 people at a concert ❿ asked to rate their responses to a variety of pieces of music, some of which were accompanied by infrasonic parts. 22 % of the participants reported feelings of anxiety, uneasiness, extreme sorrow, fear and chills down the spine, ⓫ correlated with the infrasonic events.

❶ ☐ to low	❷ ☐ with	❸ ☐ in general
☐ too low	☐ from	☐ generally
☐ much lower	☐ by	☐ general
☐ the lowest	☐ through	☐ by general
❹ ☐ on	❺ ☐ becomes	❻ ☐ experiment
☐ of	☐ became	☐ expertise
☐ from	☐ gets	☐ experiences
☐ to	☐ went	☐ exercise

❼ ☐ if ☐ as if ☐ when ☐ which	❽ ☐ mustn't ☐ will ☐ can ☐ needn't	❾ ☐ had known ☐ have been known ☐ had been known ☐ did know
❿ ☐ was ☐ where ☐ were ☐ have	⓫ ☐ as ☐ with ☐ which ☐ who	

D Text Production

Choose one of the following tasks and write about 150 words.
Count your words and write the number at the end of the text.

25 pts.

How about Newcastle?

You would like to take part in your school's exchange programme with a high school in Newcastle. As there are many more applications than places, your teacher wants all the applicants to write a text about themselves in English so that it will be easier for him to decide who will be allowed to go.

Give your **name and age** and write about at least **four** of the following aspects:
- Why would you like to take part in the exchange programme?
- Have you ever been to an English-speaking country (and if so, where)?
- What do you like to do in your free time?
- What is your family like?
- What would you show your exchange partner if he/she visited you in Germany?

or

An email to the Rocky Mountains Tourist Information Center

You are planning to visit the Rocky Mountains in Colorado in the summer. Although you have found useful information on the internet, you still need some advice.

Write an email to the local tourist information office and ask for help. Please remember to include at least **four** of the following points:
- say who you are,
- say what you want to do in the summer,
- ask for some advice on accommodation,
- ask whether there are guided (hiking) tours,
- ask how you can get there.

**Hessen Realschule – Englisch
Jahrgang 2017**

Listening Comprehension – Transcripts

Hello, this is the listening exam. I am going to give you the instructions for the test. There are three parts to the listening exam. At the beginning of each part you'll hear this sound: ◄
You may write down your answers at any point during the listening exam.

Part One

In part one you will hear two news items. You will hear the news items twice. Before listening to each news item, you will have 20 seconds to read the tasks. You now have 20 seconds to read the tasks for news item one. *(20 seconds break)* You are now going to hear the first news item for the first time. After a short break, you will hear the news item again. ◄

News Item 1: World's longest pizza

On May 19th 2016, 250 bakers of traditional Neapolitan pizza gathered in Naples to create the world's "longest" pizza. The delicious pizza was an impressive 1,850 metres long.

It took the pizza chefs 11 hours to prepare the record-breaking pizza and they used 2,000 kg of flour, 1,600 kg of tomatoes, 1,950 kg of cheese, and 200 litres of olive oil.

While the recent battle between the chefs focused on creating the world's "longest" pizza, the title for the world's "largest" has remained uncontested since 2012. Called "Ottavia", in honor of the first Roman emperor Octavian Augustus, it measured 40 metres in diameter and weighed almost 26,000 kilos! It was topped with 5,000 kilos of tomato sauce, 4,400 kilos of mozzarella cheese, and, to the disappointment of meat-lovers worldwide, 110 kilos of lettuce! Though that may seem like a strange topping choice, it made perfect sense given that Ottavia was also 100 % gluten-free and baked not just to break a record, but also to educate people about the importance of making healthy food choices.

Adapted from: http://www.dogonews.com/2016/6/5/italian-chefs-break-yet-another-guinness-world-record-for-worlds-longest-pizza

You now have 20 seconds to read the tasks for news item two. *(20 seconds break)* You are now going to hear the second news item for the first time. After a short break, you will hear news item two again. ◄

News Item 2: The first pizza delivery robot

What is more exciting than having a fresh hot pizza delivered to your door? How about having it brought to you by a robot? Thanks to CARLO's Pizza Robotic Unit or CRU, that has just become reality! On March 8th, the three-foot tall robot delivered its first pizza to some lucky residents in Brisbane, Australia.

CRU's waterproof acrylic plastic exterior protects the food from the elements, while its aluminium and steel interior ensures that the pizzas remain piping hot! The robot can deliver up to ten pizzas and even has a separate cold area to accommodate drinks orders.

Equipped with both Google Maps and GPS-guidance, CRU can find the most efficient way to its destination.

To get their food, customers have to enter a code. This not only ensures that the right pizzas are delivered, it also prevents them from being stolen.

Bruce Phelps of CARLO's Pizza Australia is confident that one day his delivery robots will become a part of daily life. We certainly can't wait!

Adapted from: http://www.dogonews.com/2016/4/3/meet-dru-the-worlds-first-pizza-delivery-robot

Part Two

> In part two a reporter is carrying out a survey. You will hear this twice. Before listening, you will have 40 seconds to read the task. You now have 40 seconds to read the task. *(40 seconds break)*
> You are now going to hear the survey for the first time. After a short break, you will hear the survey again. ◂

Survey: For or against school uniforms?

1 REPORTER: Hello, my name is Jess Banfield and I'm a journalist for the newspaper *The Birmingham Post*. Today I'm reporting from the Bullring Centre here in central Birmingham and our topic is school uniform. What do today's shoppers think? Are they for wearing a uniform in schools or against it? Let's start with you.

JANET: Me? My name is Janet and I go to Kingsbury School, just down the road. I love my school, it's got a great reputation and the teachers are alright. I'm really lucky to go to Kingsbury and I wear my uniform with pride. It makes me feel as if I belong somewhere and that I am part of a team.

MAX: Yeah, I agree with Janet, but uniforms bring other advantages too. Oh, my name is Max, by the way. I think people get a better first impression of the school if the pupils all look the same. That's certainly true at our school, anyway. It also makes it difficult for gangs, which is good. If you are in a gang, you want to stand out, wear your own colours, and so on. That's just not possible if you have to wear a uniform.

KATE: My name is Kate and I can't stand uniforms! I hate mine. It takes away my freedom to express myself as I want to. Do you think I would choose to wear this disgusting colour? Believe me, it's terrible. I'm seventeen and my mum keeps telling me, "You've got to start making your own choices now!" and then I'm not even allowed to wear what I want. It's like being in the army, where they just don't want you to think independently!

ROBERT: I'm Robert and I only partly agree with Kate. I actually like wearing uniform because it saves me time in the morning. I don't have to think about what I'm going to wear, I just reach into my wardrobe and pull out one of the school polo shirts, pull on the trousers and then I'm almost done! That's so much easier. It also means that my own clothes won't get dirty or worn out in school. They're obviously a lot more expensive.

AMIR: Hi, my name is Amir. I go to King Edward's School, which is a boys' independent school. It's pretty posh and most of the students come from rich families. I got a scholarship to go to King Edward's and we live in a normal working-class part of Birmingham. I sometimes have real problems when I come home from school. My uniform tells everyone that I go to a school for kids with lots of money. I think a lot of people, other school kids, for example, are jealous. I've often been called names on the bus on the way home.

MR GARLAND: My name is David Garland and I'm a teacher, actually. We didn't use to have a uniform at the school where I work, but the parents wanted to have one, so it was introduced. I have noticed that the pupils concentrate a lot better on their schoolwork now. Especially the girls. There are fewer conversations at the start of the day about Kevin's expensive trainers, Stacey's fashionable new jeans and Gavin's designer shirt. That's one thing I am glad about!

MR SLATER: My name is Mr Slater and I'm against school uniforms. There isn't really any evidence that uniforms improve students' results. I think it takes away time and energy from finding serious answers to problems in education. We should be concentrating on smaller classes, better security in schools, more parental help and improved facilities. These are things which would really make a difference, not whether the students are wearing a tie or not.

REPORTER: Thank you, everyone, for taking part in this survey.

Adapted from: http://school-uniforms.procon.org/

Part Three

> In part three you will hear an interview. You will hear the interview twice. Before listening to the interview, you will have 30 seconds to read the task. You now have 30 seconds to read the task.
> *(30 seconds break)* You are now going to hear the interview for the first time. After a short break, you will hear the interview again. ◀

Interview: A heroic cat

1 REPORTER: Good morning, listeners! Today our guest in the breakfast studio is Claire Hopkinson, who has brought along her cat, Tink. Now, Claire, Tink is a real hero, isn't she?

5 CLAIRE: Yes, that's right. She saved my family and me from a fire at our home.

REPORTER: What happened?

CLAIRE: Early one morning last February, I was fast asleep in bed when I was suddenly woken up by Tink, who had jumped up onto my legs. This was very unusual because she sleeps downstairs and she never comes into the bedroom.

REPORTER: OK.

15 CLAIRE: I sat up feeling terrible – I had been out the night before, but I soon realised something was very wrong. The room was half-filled with a layer of white smoke hanging in the air. It was quite creepy.

20 REPORTER: Yes, I bet! Go on.

CLAIRE: Well, I woke my partner, Russ, in a panic and we both jumped out of bed. Our two boys had woken up too and there was black smoke blowing out of their room. It was already difficult to breathe. I phoned the fire brigade, who told us to leave the house as soon as possible.

REPORTER: Oh, that must have been scary!

CLAIRE: Yes, it was. We thought that Tink had already escaped from the house too. Anyways, within seven minutes, six fire engines arrived and as I stood looking at our house, I realised that the source of the fire was actually our next-door neighbour's. The flames were licking the front of her house. For half an hour, the firefighters sprayed our two houses with water until the fire was out. At that point, however, we were getting worried about Tink. There was no sign of her anywhere.

40 REPORTER: Did you go back into the house to look for her?

CLAIRE: No, we didn't, but we told a firefighter and he went back in. After a few moments, he came back out with Tink lying in his arms. Tink wasn't breathing and her tongue was hanging out.

REPORTER: Where did the firefighter find her?

CLAIRE: She was lying behind a cupboard in the kitchen. When I saw her, I burst into tears! I thought she was dead! The firefighter put an oxygen mask on her and incredibly, she took a breath and coughed.

REPORTER: Oh, what a relief!

CLAIRE: Yes, it was amazing! She stank of smoke and was very dirty, but she was alive.

REPORTER: So what did you do the following morning?

CLAIRE: Well, we now had nowhere to live, so Tink went to my sister's and we stayed in a hotel for one month. It took us weeks to recover from this trauma. One corner of our house had been burnt and our things were ruined. I was especially upset because we had lost all our photographs. When we went to visit my sister, it was clear that Tink had suffered too. She was timid and frightened. She refused to get off my knees when I tried to get up.

REPORTER: Oh, dear!

CLAIRE: Yes. However, we have now moved into a rented accommodation while our house is being renovated and Tink has finally come back to us.

REPORTER: And she looks very healthy and happy now, don't you, Tinks? *(Miaow!)* What an amazing story. Cats are not generally known for their heroic actions.

CLAIRE: Yes, Tink's sixth sense saved our lives, she really is an exception!

Adapted from: https://www.theguardian.com/lifeandstyle/2016/jul/15/my-cat-saved-me-from-fire-experience

> You may now continue with the rest of the exam. Good luck!

Abschlussprüfung Englisch 2017

A Listening Comprehension

Part One

Listen to the news items and tick (✓) the right statements.
There is only one possible answer per statement.

News Item 1: World's longest pizza   4 pts.

a) The world's longest pizza is
   ____ metres long
   - [ ] 250
   - [x] 1,850
   - [ ] 2,000

b) The chefs used ____ kg of cheese
   - [ ] 200
   - [ ] 1,600
   - [x] 1,950

c) The record for the world's largest pizza was set in
   - [ ] 2000.
   - [x] 2012.
   - [ ] 2016.

d) The "Ottavia" was topped with
   - [ ] meat.
   - [ ] olive oil.
   - [x] lettuce.

News Item 2: The first pizza delivery robot   4 pts.

a) The new pizza delivery robot is called
   - [x] Carlo.
   - [x] CRU.
   - [ ] Robotic Unit.

b) The exterior of the robot is made of
   - [x] plastic.
   - [ ] aluminium.
   - [ ] steel.

c) The robot can
   - [ ] order drinks.
   - [ ] make hot pizzas.
   - [x] keep drinks cool.

d) In order to get the right pizza, the buyer must
   - [x] type in a number.
   - [ ] order it from the robot.
   - [ ] pick up the right one.

Part Two

Survey: For or against school uniforms?

Listen to these people talking about school uniforms.
Who thinks what? Write the correct letters in the chart.
Be careful – there is one statement more than you need.

7 pts.

A A uniform stops me from being who I want to be.

B A uniform gives me a positive feeling of belonging.

C Some people are prejudiced when they see my uniform.

D Wearing a uniform means I can just get up in the morning and go.

E There is less chat in the classroom now.

F I'm in a gang and wearing a uniform makes it harder for me to stand out.

G We should be concentrating on more serious problems in schools, not on clothes.

H Visitors to my school are impressed by our uniform.

Janet	Max	Kate	Robert	Amir	Mr Garland	Mr Slater
B	H	A	D	C	E	G

Part Three

Interview: A heroic cat

Listen to the interview and write down the information needed.
Fill in only one detail per box.

10 pts.

why Claire woke up	Tink jumped on her legs ~~Tink woke her up~~
how she realised something was wrong	by white smoke
what she did next	woke her partner up
where the fire had started	~~The~~ neighbors
Tink's condition after her rescue	~~She~~ Tink was unconcious
Tink's hiding place in the kitchen during the fire	Behind a cupboard in the kitchen
what the firefighter did for Tink	Put a gasmash on Tink
why Claire was particularly upset after the fire	Because she thought Tink had died
how Tink behaved after the fire	Frightend
where they live now	~~accomidation~~ accomidation

B Reading Comprehension

1. What about a handshake?

❶ After living in Germany for about 12 months, an Englishman returns to London to visit his parents. When he greets his father, he does something he has never done before in his whole life – he shakes his father's hand. He has picked up the German habit of shaking hands with strangers, colleagues, friends – and family. In a small way, he has become German.

❷ It's not that British people don't shake hands. They do, generally, when they meet someone for the first time. But they don't shake hands again at the end of the day, or at dinner time, or early the next morning, or at the next meeting – nor do they shake hands with their parents, even if they haven't seen them for a while.

❸ Handshaking is a universal greeting that has been around for thousands of years. Originally, people shook hands to show that they were unarmed and didn't want to hurt anyone. Although we now shake hands simply because it is a custom, the way we grip can still tell a lot about our character or attitude. In the first moments of meeting, somebody creates a basis for the relationship that follows. A "limp fish" handshake and a "knuckle-crusher" can make equally negative impressions on a business partner or even on a future spouse. What do we really want to communicate in the first moments of meeting someone? Strength? Self-confidence? Control? Friendliness? Probably a little of all these things – and our handshake can support this.

❹ When greeting Britons and Americans, make sure your handshake is firm but not aggressive – three or four seconds is enough; shorter is too timid, and longer too intrusive. While shaking, try to make eye contact, smile, say your name and (in business) your position. Avoid old-fashioned introductory phrases such as "Delighted to make your acquaintance", which sound as if they are from a textbook. On the other hand, there are still people who use the expression "How do you do?". Just remember that the answer is also "How do you do?".

❺ And what about gender differences? It used to be the rule that women remained seated, and men waited for the lady to offer her hand. Now that women have equal rights, why should they shake hands any differently? The real fun starts in multicultural situations. It may be more appropriate to hug in Paris or to bow in Tokyo, and some women in Vienna may still appreciate having their hand kissed. In a foreign country, we need to know about local customs and how to use them. To the younger generation, high fives and 'gangsta' greetings may seem cool, but in business circles, the traditional handshake will be the greeting of choice for quite a while to come.

From: Spotlight 4/2010, p. 59

Match the five correct headings to each part of the text (1–5).
Be careful – there are two headings more than you need. 5 pts.

A	A HANDSHAKE SAYS MORE THAN A 1000 WORDS
B	HOW TO DO A "KNUCKLE-CRUSHER"
C	HANDSHAKE ETIQUETTE ALL AROUND THE WORLD
D	LIVING ABROAD CAN CHANGE HOW YOU GREET
E	HIGH FIVES IN BUSINESS CIRCLES
F	WHEN TO SHAKE HANDS IN THE UK
G	DO'S AND DON'TS IN HANDSHAKES

part of the text	❶	❷	❸	❹	❺
heading					

2. **Fun in mines**

Once underground mines have served their purpose, most are sealed and forgotten. The approximately 1000-year-old salt mine in the city of Turda, Romania, was no exception. The mine, which is believed to have opened in the Middle Ages (as far back as 1075), was shut in 1932 after competition from neighbouring mines rendered its operation unprofitable.

In 1939 during World War Two, its massive underground caverns were used as bomb shelters for the residents of Turda. When the war drew to an end in 1945, local cheese makers decided to use the mine's naturally cool and dark interior for storing cheese.

This continued until 1992, when the city's officials came up with the brilliant idea of turning the historical salt mine into a museum for adults and an amusement park for kids. The theme park, which has been visited by over 2.5 million people since its opening, is now ranked 22nd among the world's most spectacular destinations.

Visitors to the theme park are transported 400 metres underground in the same elevator shafts that were used to bring excavated salt to the surface over a century ago. Here lies an amusement park like none other – one that includes a giant Ferris wheel, a minigolf course, tennis courts and even an underground lake that can be navigated using paddle boats.

The mine even has a 180 seat amphitheatre for concerts and conferences as well as a swimming pool and spa for those that want a relaxing experience underground.

Adults and kids can learn about the history of the mine while admiring the perfectly preserved salt extracting equipment in the museum. There are other sections, for example the

20 Terezia mine. In the interior of the cone-shaped mine that lies an astounding 112 metres underground, guests will find lots of stalactites along with a magical lake.

But the Turda salt mine is not the only mine transformation. In North Wales, the Llechwedd slate quarry has been converted into a trampoline paradise with over 3,000 square metres of netting. These are suspended 6, 18, and 24 metres above the ground and connected by a net-
25 work of spiral staircases or slides illuminated by multi-coloured lights.

In Missouri, the Bonne Terre Mine boasts the seventeen-mile-long "Billion Gallon Lake". Visitors can take walking tours around what is believed to be the world's largest freshwater dive resort, rent boats to traverse through the various passages or even scuba dive in the crystal clear waters.

30 Those looking for a more traditional mining experience can head to the Consolidated Gold Mine in Dahlonega, Georgia. Here they will get an opportunity to learn how the ancient miners lived and also experience their day first-hand by panning for gold or mining for gems. Who knew there is so much entertainment hidden underground?

Adapted from: https://www.dogonews.com/2016/3/20/romanias-historical-salina-turda-salt-mine-is-home-to-a-unique-underground-amusement-park

Tick (✓) the right statements. There is only one possible answer per statement. 10 pts.

a) The Turda salt mine was closed for mining in
- [ ] 1932.
- [ ] 1939.
- [ ] 1945.
- [ ] 1992.

b) It was closed because
- [ ] mines nearby were more lucrative.
- [ ] it was needed as a bomb shelter.
- [ ] a cheese factory bought it.
- [ ] the city wanted to have a museum.

c) Today, the Turda salt mine is
- [ ] used to excavate salt.
- [ ] a huge golf course.
- [ ] a popular theme park.
- [ ] a trampoline paradise.

d) The mine is also in ____ place of the world's most amazing locations.
- [ ] twentieth
- [ ] twenty-second
- [ ] sixtieth
- [ ] one hundred and twelfth

e) In the park, you can
- [ ] play tennis, use paddle boats and jump on trampolines.
- [ ] swim, play tennis and go on a Ferris wheel.
- [ ] play minigolf, go on a Ferris wheel and take guided walking tours.

f) In the Turda salt mine, people can admire tools of the past
- [ ] in the museum.
- [ ] in the Terezia mine.
- [ ] in the cone-shaped mine.
- [ ] on the magical lake.

g) The Llechwedd slate quarry features 3,000 square metres of
- [ ] slides.
- [ ] staircases.
- [ ] freshwater.
- [ ] bouncing nets.

h) Unlike the other mines, the Bonne Terre Mine offers
- [ ] a seventeen mile walk.
- [ ] scuba-diving in saltwater.
- [ ] scuba-diving in freshwater.
- [ ] walking tours underwater.

i) The special feature of the mine in Dahlonega is that
- [ ] people can look for gems.
- [ ] one can see how miners now live.
- [ ] it is a multi-coloured mining experience.
- [ ] you traverse a gold passage.

k) You could enjoy a choir concert in the
- [ ] Llechwedd slate quarry.
- [ ] Turda salt mine.
- [ ] Bonne Terre Mine.
- [ ] Consolidated Gold Mine.

3. The Film Club

In the following extract, Jesse, a fifteen-year-old American teenager, introduces a girl to his father, David, who tells what happens from his point of view.

1 One day he brought a girl home. Her name was Rebecca Ng, a Vietnamese knockout. [...]

Rebecca Ng (pronounced Ning) was dressed to the nines[1], spotless white jeans, maroon, long-collared blouse, leather jacket, Beatle boots. [...] As she turned her head to speak to Jesse, I caught a whiff of perfume: delicate, expensive.

5 "So here we are," she said.

Then he took her downstairs to his bedroom. I opened my mouth to protest. It was a pit down there. There were no windows, no natural light. Just a bed with a ratty green blanket, clothes on the floor, CDs splashed around the room, a computer facing the wall, a "library" consisting of an autographed Elmore Leonard (unread), George Elliot's *Middlemarch* (a
10 hopeful gift from his mother), plus a collection of hip-hop magazines with scowling black men on the covers. A collection of water glasses squatted on the night table. They cracked like a pistol shot when you prised[2] them loose. [...]

Soon the whump of a bass guitar rose up through the floor. You could hear Rebecca's voice floating above the music, then Jesse's voice, deeper, confident. Then bright bursts of laugh-
15 ter. Good, I thought, she's discovered how amusing he is.

"How *old* is that girl?" I asked when he returned from walking her to the subway.

"Sixteen," he said. "She's got a boyfriend, though."

"I can imagine."

He smiled uncertainly. "What do you mean?"

20 "Nothing in particular."

He looked worried.

I said, "I suppose I mean that if she's got a boyfriend, why is she over at your house?"

"She's pretty, isn't she?"

"She certainly is. She knows it too." [...]

25 He caught a glimpse of himself in the mirror over the kitchen sink. Turning his head slightly to the side, he sucked in his cheeks, pursed his lips and frowned gravely. This was his "mirror face". A way he never looked otherwise. You almost expected his hair, which was thick like a raccoon's, to stand up on end.

"But the guy before him was twenty-five," he said. Clearly, he wanted to talk about her. Pul-
30 ling his eyes with some difficulty from his reflection, his face returned to its normal cast.

"Twenty-five?"

"She's got guys all over her, Dad. Like flies."

In that instant he seemed wiser than I was at his age. Less delusionally vain; hardly an accomplishment. But the whole thing with Rebecca Ng made me nervous. It was like watching
35 him get into a very expensive car. You could smell the new leather from here.

"I didn't look like I was coming on to her or anything, did I?" he asked.

"No, not at all."

"Not nervous or anything?"

"No. Were you?"

40 "Just when I look closely at her. The rest of the time I'm fine."

"You seemed pretty on top of things to me."

"I did, didn't I?"

Adapted from: David Gilmour: The Film Club, Twelve 2007, p. 17–21

1 dressed to the nines = dressed really smartly, very well-dressed
2 prise = loosen something with force

Answer the questions.

a) Describe Rebecca's style.   1 pt.

___

b) Why does David, Jesse's dad, want to protest when Jesse takes Rebecca downstairs?   1 pt.

___

c) What are Jesse and Rebecca doing in Jesse's room? (two details)   2 pts.

___

___

d) What does Jesse tell his father about Rebecca's relationships with boys?   1 pt.

___

e) What does Jesse do when he makes his "mirror face"?   1 pt.

___

f) David realizes that Jesse behaves differently to him at that age. How is Jesse's behaviour different?   1 pt.

___

g) How does Jesse feel when he is with Rebecca? 1 pt.

You cannot find the answers to the following questions directly in the text:

h) What does Jesse's dad mean when he calls Rebecca a knockout? 1 pt.

i) Why does Jesse ask his dad what he thinks about his behaviour towards Rebecca? 1 pt.

C Use of Language

1. **Mediation** 11 pts.

    The school mediators

    An deiner Schule gibt es in diesem Jahr eine Austauschschülerin. In ihrer ersten Woche an eurer Schule sieht sie auf dem Schulhof zwei Schüler, die rote Pullover tragen. Leider spricht sie kaum Deutsch, und die beiden Schüler sprechen noch nicht so gut Englisch. Du stehst in der Nähe und bietest deine Hilfe an.

    Vermittle zwischen der Austauschschülerin Claire und den beiden deutschen Schülern Markus und Thomas. Ergänze den folgenden Dialog mit den wichtigsten Informationen in der jeweils geforderten Sprache.

    CLAIRE: Hey you two. Why are you wearing those red pullovers?

    DU [DEUTSCH]: _____ 1 pt.

    MARKUS: Hallo Claire. Wir sind die Streitschlichter an dieser Schule, und so können uns die anderen als Streitschlichter erkennen. Außerdem gefällt uns die Farbe.

    DU [ENGLISCH]: _____ 2 pts.

CLAIRE:	Oh, I understand. And what exactly is your task? We don't have anything like that at our school. And by the way, German and American schools are so different!
DU [DEUTSCH]:	_____ 2 pts.
THOMAS:	Wir helfen Schülerinnen und Schülern, wenn sie Streit miteinander haben, eine Lösung für ihren Konflikt zu finden. Egal, ob Jungs oder Mädchen, Jüngere oder Ältere.
DU [ENGLISCH]:	_____ 1 pt.
CLAIRE:	Really, and how did you learn that?
DU [DEUTSCH]:	_____ 1 pt.
MARKUS:	Wir haben an zwei Wochenenden ein spezielles Training mitgemacht. Dabei haben wir in Rollenspielen gelernt, wie man mit Schülerinnen und Schülern spricht. Am Ende gab es dann sogar einen kleinen Test. Das war ganz schön anstrengend, aber es hat sich gelohnt. Außerdem waren wir in einer tollen Jugendherberge, mit eigenem Schwimmbad. Das war wirklich super.
DU [ENGLISCH]:	_____ 2 pts.
CLAIRE:	Wow, that sounds really great. Can I come to your next meeting?
DU [DEUTSCH]:	_____ 1 pt.
THOMAS:	Ja, natürlich, wir treffen uns jeden ersten Donnerstag im Monat. Es gibt auch immer Kuchen und Limonade.
DU [ENGLISCH]:	_____ 1 pt.
CLAIRE:	Well, that sounds really interesting. Thanks for the chat. Bye.
MARKUS:	Bitte, tschüss!

2. Words and structures

Faces of India

Read the text, then choose the correct words from the box to fill in the gaps.
Use each word once only. There are more words than you need.
Be careful – some gaps are at the beginning of the sentence.

14 pts.

> call • continue • fascinating • fastest • for • hardships •
> has • highly • in • land • live • living • much • off • one •
> since • state • surprisingly • tending • will

India is an exciting country, with the Himalayas in the north and the paradise of Goa's beaches in the south. The tourist (1) _____ also find history and culture in the capital, New Delhi, and colourful nightlife and the Bollywood vibe in Mumbai, (2) _____ of India's most fascinating cities.

(3) _____ eighty-nine years, India was the "jewel in the crown" of the British Empire. That's why English – along with Hindi – is one of India's two major official languages. India has been an independent democracy (4) _____ 1947 – the biggest on the planet.

Today, with more than a billion people, India has one of the world's (5) _____ growing economies. Information technology, (6) _____ -centres and tourism are big business. Education is very important to produce the (7) _____ qualified workers India needs.

Bollywood, the centre of India's film industry, makes around 900 films a year – and Indian music and dance, which are a big part of the films, (8) _____ to be very popular. But that's not surprising because India has one of the youngest populations (9) _____ the world.

Rajasthan is a (10) _____ in north-western India. Here people still (11) _____ in mud-walled homes with no electricity or running water. Many children go to school, but others stay home to work, carrying water and firewood, (12) _____ livestock and minding younger children.

Despite the (13) _____, the villagers are extremely kind and generous and share chai (tea) or roti (bread) with every visitor.

Regardless where you go, India is a colourful and (14) _____ place.

From: Spot On, 8/2009, pp. 10–15

D Text Production

Choose one of the following tasks and write about 150 words.
Count your words and write the number at the end of the text.

25 pts.

What is the story behind the picture?

The online travel magazine which you often read publishes unusual holiday photos. You took this picture on your last holiday and you decide to submit it.

Write an e-mail to go with the photo and include at least **four** of the following aspects:
- Who are these people?
- Where have they come from?
- Why are they there?
- What will they do next?
- Why did you take the picture?

© REUTERS/China Stringer Network

___
or
___

The perfect end-of-school party

You want to write an article about what makes a perfect end-of-school party for the online magazine of your English partner school. Think about the different possibilities of how to organize the festivities and give reasons for your preferred choice.

Write an article and include at least **four** of the following aspects:
- location
- food
- music
- programme
- style

**Hessen Realschule – Englisch
Jahrgang 2018**

Listening Comprehension – Transcripts

Hello, this is the listening exam. I am going to give you the instructions for the test. There are three parts to the listening exam. At the beginning of each part you'll hear this sound: ◀
You may write down your answers at any point during the listening exam.

Part One

In part one you will hear two news items. You will hear the news items twice. Before listening to each news item, you will have 20 seconds to read the tasks. You now have 20 seconds to read the tasks for news item one. *(20 seconds break)* You are now going to hear the first news item for the first time. After a short break, you will hear the news item again. ◀

News Item 1: Smart translator *The Pilot*

Imagine being able to visit any foreign country without having to worry about the language. Until recently, translating devices only existed in science fiction movies. But companies worldwide are working feverishly to introduce universal translators. Among them is the New York start-up company, Waverly Labs.
Their solution, called *The Pilot*, is a smart earpiece that instantly translates spoken language. The device, an in-ear headphone, picks up the sound of the speech, which then goes through a smartphone app that "whispers" it back to the listener in his or her own language. As a result, the user is able to understand the other person despite not knowing the language.
Currently, the device is dependent on having a data connection, but developers hope that future generations of *The Pilot* will function offline too. *The Pilot* can only translate one-on-one conversations. However, researchers at Waverly Labs are confident that it will soon be able to translate everything that is going on around the user as well.
Preorders of *The Pilot Translating Earpieces* cost US $ 249 and come with free access to French, Italian, Spanish, along with English. Users can also purchase additional languages including Arabic, Mandarin Chinese, German, Japanese, Russian and many more. The dream of a life free of language barriers has finally become real.

Adapted from: https://www.dogonews.com/2016/10/30/smart-earpiece-translates-foreign-languages-in-real-time (last accessed on 13. 02. 2017), http://www.waverlylabs.com/pilot-translation-kit/ (last accessed on 07. 09. 2017)

You now have 20 seconds to read the tasks for news item two. *(20 seconds break)* You are now going to hear the second news item for the first time. After a short break, you will hear news item two again. ◀

News Item 2: Meet LiLou

On December 5th, San Francisco Airport officials introduced LiLou, the newest member of the Wag Brigade, a group of friendly therapy dogs that roam the airport terminals to provide comfort to travellers. However, two-year-old LiLou is not a Labrador or a Chihuahua like her colleagues, but a Juliana. At this point you are probably wondering why you have never heard of this dog breed. Let me help you – LiLou is a small and colourful pig.
The idea of LiLou becoming a therapy animal came from her owner, Tatyana Danilove.
LiLou underwent the same training as the dogs and only after she passed with flying colours was she included in this all-important Wag Brigade family that boasts 300 canine members.
LiLou wears scarlet nail polish on her perfectly manicured nails. She can greet fans, wave, or thank them with a shake of her tail and even enter-

tain them with live music on her toy piano. Airport officials say the pig even takes a bow after each performance! When not helping calm nerves at the airport, LiLou can often be found entertaining the sick at local hospitals and visiting the elderly at retirement homes.

Adapted from: https://www.dogonews.com/2016/12/11/adorable-pig-calms-stressed-travelers-at-san-francisco-airport (last accessed on 14. 02. 2017)

Part Two

> In part two a reporter is carrying out a survey. You will hear this twice. Before listening, you will have 40 seconds to read the task. You now have 40 seconds to read the task. *(40 seconds break)*
> You are now going to hear the survey for the first time. After a short break, you will hear the survey again. ◂

Survey: Modern communication

Reporter: Hello and welcome to tonight's show. Our topic this evening is texting. Almost everybody nowadays has a mobile phone and sends messages, texts and photos to friends and family. Is it all good? This morning, I asked some holidaymakers in Brighton what they thought of texting. This is what they said.

Jane: Hi, I'm Jane. Last year I spent eight months working as an au pair in the USA. At the beginning, I felt quite lonely. Making friends was really hard, but thanks to social media, I was able to keep in touch with friends at home and tell or write to them about what I was doing. This made my situation easier.

Graham: Hello, my name is Graham Burgess. Generally, I like using my phone for contacting people, but I really do get fed up when I get messages which I can hardly understand because the spelling is so bad. Yes, you may have guessed – I'm a teacher. Students write their essays like they write their text messages. It's a disaster.

Mary: My name is Mary and I'm a manager for a big retail company. I have to hold interviews and I have noticed that people find it increasingly difficult to communicate face to face. They are unable to hold eye contact and they lack the social skills they need. One reason for this is definitely too much use of social media platforms.

David: Hi. David here. I love my mobile phone and I write at least 30 messages a day. It's great. However, it does get on my nerves if I am out on a first date, for example, and the girl keeps receiving calls and texts and spends more time on her phone than talking to me.

Rebecca: My name is Rebecca. It's ironic, but I think a mobile phone, which is designed to keep people connected, can actually drive us further apart. Have you ever seen a group of friends sitting in a restaurant looking down at their phones instead of at each other? You have? That's exactly what I mean.

Mia: Hi everyone! My name's Mia. It's great being able to text a friend when you are out and about. You can quickly make a date, be spontaneous, change your mind or chat to several people at the same time. It's so convenient.

Sim: My name is Sim. I'm still at school and when I start my homework, I have to put my phone in another room. It's so tempting to pick it up and see whether my mates have started their homework, or I might arrange to meet someone or check the football scores. I really have to be strict with myself.

Reporter: Thank you for all your interesting comments.

Adapted from: http://www.importantindia.com/22926/mobile-phones-advantages-disadvantages/ (last accessed on 06. 09. 2017)

Part Three

> In part three you will hear an interview. You will hear the interview twice. Before listening to the interview, you will have 30 seconds to read the task. You now have 30 seconds to read the task.
> *(30 seconds break)* You are now going to hear the interview for the first time. After a short break, you will hear the interview again. ◂

Interview: Mom on strike

Reporter: Today on the show, my guest is Jessica Stilwell, an ordinary working mom who decided to teach her children an extraordinary lesson. Welcome, Jessica. Tell us your story, please. What did you do that was so special?

Jessica: I decided to go on strike.

Reporter: What do you mean?

Jessica: Well, I decided to stop tidying up after the children. It all began on October 1st, that was a Saturday and my husband Dylan was away golfing for the weekend. For me, it was a typical weekend day filled with errands and sports. I sat down for the first time at 11 am and looked around me. The house was in a real mess and none of it was from me.

Reporter: Yes, I think we all know how that feels.

Jessica: So I decided to go on strike and stop tidying and cleaning up after the children. I didn't tell the children, though. I just stopped. I did keep a blog, however, about the increasing mess.

Reporter: And with your blog, you became a real Internet star! How long did you go on strike for?

Jessica: Six days in total. At the end of the first day, the breakfast dishes and the dinner dishes were still on the table, all crusty. The dishwasher was overflowing and the children's shoes and backpacks were in the middle of the hall.

Reporter: It just shows you how quickly things can get messy. How many children do you have, Jessica?

Jessica: We have got twin girls, who are 12, and another daughter, who is 10.

Reporter: OK. And what happened next? Did the situation get better or worse?

Jessica: It got worse! At the end of Day Two, there were dirty socks on the floor and used tissues on the sofa. The cereal left sitting in the milk from the day before was starting to stink and the dog had licked clean the dirty plates in the dishwasher.

Reporter: That sounds terrible. But didn't the children notice that something was wrong?

Jessica: Yes, Quinn, my youngest daughter, when she saw the soggy cereal, said, "Eeeee! What is THAT?" But she still didn't wash the bowl or carry it to the sink. It was a hard lesson and at times I felt awful, but I didn't give in.

Reporter: Keep going, Jessica! What happened on Day Four?

Jessica: Well, Quinn broke down crying and said, "I don't want to eat off paper plates or drink out of plastic beakers! Can you please help me to clean up?" And she went around picking up her things.

Reporter: Were you starting to feel bad that your daughter was unhappy?

Jessica: Yes, I was, but I also knew that I had to keep going for another couple of days, otherwise it would have all been for nothing.

Reporter: You did really well.

Jessica: Yes, and then finally on Day Six, I stopped the strike because the children were beginning to fight and blame each other. At that point, we all sat down on the sofa and talked. Then they apologized to me and started to clean up.

Reporter: How long did that take?

Jessica: It took them two days and I didn't do a thing, I just sat on the couch and drank coffee which my daughters had made for me. The girls complained bitterly, but they kept at it, and eventually, the whole house was nearly perfect.

Reporter: Wow! And what is it like now? Have they learned their lesson?

Jessica: Yes, mostly. They do now rinse their breakfast dishes and put them in the dishwasher and they empty their lunchboxes from the day before.

Reporter: You must be proud of yourself. You have made them more independent. When they leave home one day, they will be able to look after themselves.

Jessica: Let's hope so. Nobody's perfect, though. This morning I found a pair of dirty socks on the stairs.

Reporter: As you say, Jessica, nobody's perfect.

Adapted from: http://www.huffingtonpost.com/2012/10/08/jessica-stilwell-mom-on-strike_n_1948603.html
(last accessed on 02. 07. 2017)

You may now continue with the rest of the exam. Good luck!

A Listening Comprehension

Part One

Listen to the news items and tick (✓) the right statements.
There is only one possible answer per statement.

News Item 1: Smart translator *The Pilot*   4 pts.

a) *The Pilot* can translate what you
- [ ] write.
- [ ] say.
- [ ] read.

b) At the moment, the device works
- [ ] only online.
- [ ] only offline.
- [ ] online and offline.

c) *The Pilot* translates
- [ ] background conversation.
- [ ] group conversations.
- [ ] conversation between two people.

d) These languages are free with *The Pilot Translating Earpieces*:
- [ ] French, Italian, Spanish and English
- [ ] Arabic, Japanese, German and English
- [ ] Russian, German, English and Arabic

News Item 2: Meet LiLou   4 pts.

a) LiLou is a
- [ ] Labrador.
- [ ] Juliana.
- [ ] Chihuahua.

b) She is a
- [ ] dog.
- [ ] traveller.
- [ ] pig.

c) LiLou has
- [ ] painted nails.
- [ ] a toy guitar.
- [ ] a bow on her tail.

d) When not at the airport, LiLou can often be found
- [ ] at training facilities.
- [ ] flying.
- [ ] in hospitals.

Part Two

Survey: Modern communication

Listen to these people talking about texting.
Who thinks what? Write the correct letters in the chart.
Be careful – there is one statement more than you need.

7 pts.

A Too much texting can effect your behaviour in a job situation.

B Mobile phones can make you isolated instead of bringing people together.

C It annoys me when people can't write properly.

D I get at least thirty messages a day.

E Messaging makes me flexible.

F Messaging helped me through a difficult time.

G You should leave your phone at home if you are meeting someone for the first time.

H My phone can be a distraction.

Jane	Graham	Mary	David	Rebecca	Mia	Sim

Part Three

Interview: Mom on strike

Listen to the interview and write down the information needed.
Fill in only only one detail per box.

10 pts.

what Jessica means by 'going on strike'	
why this was necessary	
what was wrong in the house (2 aspects)	
what the dog did	
what happened on Day Four	
why Jessica ended the strike	
what she did while the children were tidying up	
what the children now do to help	
why Jessica can feel proud of herself	

B Reading Comprehension

1. **Tennis star Andy Murray and the science of success**

    ❶ If you want to know what it is about Andy Murray that makes him stand out from the rest of us, it is summed up in two words – osmolarity check. This is a test where the percentages of water and minerals in his urine are measured, to show whether his body is correctly hydrated. Andy Murray's success is due mostly to science. There is nothing in his life that is left to chance, nothing that isn't measured, calibrated and balanced.

    ❷ Take his diet. Murray will start the day with yogurt, fruit and a bagel smeared with peanut butter. On his way to the All England Tennis Club he will nibble at a protein bar and a banana. Ninety minutes before his match, he will have a plateful of chicken and rice, loaded with energy-delivering protein. Then, afterwards, there will be sushi; he eats up to fifty pieces a day. The mix of protein and carbohydrate without a hint of fat is reckoned to be the perfect way to recover physical resources after an intense physical workout.

    ❸ And all the while he will be drinking. Murray is rarely seen without a bottle in his hand (not alcohol: he is a life-long teetotaler). On court, between games, he sips at a cloudy, lemon-coloured liquid. Mixed by his nutritionist, it's a formula of glucose, sodium, potassium and other minerals that help sustain his energy and concentration levels. He takes a packet of it in powder form wherever he goes, adding to the water supplied. He doesn't drink fizzy water, though. This interferes with his digestion.

    ❹ Murray has not arrived at this sort of regime by chance. He employs experts to tell him what is best in every area of his physical development. Six people spend their lives assessing and checking his body. There is his coach and his practice partner, two fitness experts and two physiotherapists who attend to his recovery after matches. Immediately after he comes off court, the pair will be at work. They will supervise his ice bath and then start the massage. This is nothing like we might enjoy in a spa hotel. It is a deep muscle manipulation using elbows and knuckles.

    ❺ But perhaps the most effective scientific application has been on the muscle between Murray's ears. Previously, he believed that sports psychologists could not tell him anything of any use. But since eight-time grand slam winner Ivan Lendl became his coach, the difference he has made to Murray's mental preparation has been significant. The crowd at Wimbledon – and the ten million watching on television – may have been dizzy with the drama of what they had just witnessed. But the man himself was calm and restrained in the press conference. Scientific analysis has taught him that you do not waste your energy. Murray is just doing his job.

Adapted from: Jim White: Andy Murray's appliance of science, 04. 07. 2013, http://www.telegraph.co.uk/sport/tennis/andymurray/ 10159973/Andy-Murrays-appliance-of-science.html (last accessed on 05. 01. 2017)

Match the five correct headings to each part of the text (1–5).
Be careful – there are two headings more than you need. 5 pts.

A	BACKGROUND TEAM
B	PSYCHOLOGICAL DIFFERENCE
C	BEAUTY SPA TREATMENTS
D	DIETARY REQUIREMENTS
E	SPECIAL COCKTAIL MIX
F	BREAKFAST HABITS
G	FLUID ANALYSIS

part of the text	❶	❷	❸	❹	❺
heading					

2. Toxic e-waste dumped in poor nations

Millions of mobile phones, laptops, tablets, toys, digital cameras and other electronic devices bought this Christmas can create a flood of dangerous electronic waste (e-waste) that is being dumped illegally in developing countries, the UN has warned.

The global volume of electronic waste is expected to grow by 33 percent in the next four years, when it will weigh the equivalent of eight of the great Egyptian pyramids, the UN has declared. Last year, nearly 50 million tonnes of e-waste were generated worldwide – or about seven kilograms for every person on the planet. These are electronic goods made up of hundreds of different materials and containing toxic substances such as lead, mercury, cadmium and arsenic. An old-style computer screen can contain up to three kilograms of lead, for example.

Once in a landfill, these toxic materials seep out into the environment, polluting land, water and the air. In addition, electronic devices are often dismantled in primitive conditions. Those who work at these sites suffer frequently from illness.

According to Ruediger Kuehr, from the UN, "The increase in e-waste is happening because there's so much technical innovation. TVs, mobile phones and computers are all being replaced more and more quickly. The lifetime of products is also shortening."

The UN reports that e-waste – which extends from old fridges to toys and even motorized toothbrushes – is now the world's fastest growing waste stream. China produced 11.1 million tonnes in 2015, followed by the US with 10 million tonnes, though there was a significant difference per person. For example, on average each American produced 29.5 kilograms, compared to less than five kilograms per person in China.

In Europe, Germany throws away the most e-waste in total, but Norway and Liechtenstein throw away more per person. Britain is now the world's seventh largest producer, throwing away 1.37 million tonnes, or about 21 kilograms per person.

25 A new study by the Massachusetts Institute of Technology suggests that the US threw away 258.2 million computers, monitors, TVs and mobile phones in 2015, of which only 66 percent were recycled. Nearly 120 million mobile phones were collected, most of which were shipped to Hong Kong, Latin America and the Caribbean. On average a mobile phone is used for less than two years, but the EU, US and Japanese governments say many hundreds
30 of millions are thrown away each year or are left in drawers. In the US, only 12 million mobile phones were collected for recycling in 2016, even though 120 million were bought. Meanwhile, newer phone models are racing on to the market leaving old ones likely to end up in landfills.

Most phones contain precious metals. The circuit board can contain copper, gold, zinc and
35 others. The coatings are typically made of lead and phone makers are now increasingly using lithium batteries. Yet fewer than 10 percent of mobile phones are dismantled and reused. Part of the problem is that computers, phones and other devices are becoming increasingly complicated and made of smaller and smaller components.

The failure to recycle is also leading to shortages of rare-earth elements to make future gen-
40 erations of electronic equipment.

Adapted from: John Vidal: Toxic 'e-waste' dumped in poor nations, says United Nations, 14. 12. 2013,
https://www.theguardian.com/global-development/2013/dec/14/toxic-ewaste-illegal-dumping-developing-countries
(last accessed on 16. 01. 2017)

Tick (✓) the right statements. There is only one possible answer per statement. 10 pts.

a) The UN reports that electronic rubbish
- [ ] is taken to less developed countries.
- [ ] is dumped in developed countries.
- [ ] was bought this Christmas.
- [ ] has caused a flood.

b) The amount of e-waste will
- [ ] weigh as much as an Egyptian pyramid.
- [ ] be stored near the Egyptian pyramids.
- [ ] increase in the near future.
- [ ] be tackled by the UN programme.

c) Last year, ____ of e-waste were made.
- [ ] more than 50 million tonnes
- [ ] about seven million kilograms
- [ ] about 50 million tonnes
- [ ] less than seven million kilograms

d) One problem is that
- ☐ workers in Europe suffer from illness.
- ☐ poisonous substances escape into the environment.
- ☐ electronic goods contain toxic substances like copper.
- ☐ mobile phones in use pollute land, water and air.

e) Nowadays,
- ☐ electronic goods do not last long.
- ☐ technical innovation is slowing down.
- ☐ TVs and mobile phones pollute the environment.
- ☐ TVs and mobile phones explode.

f) In 2015, ____ produced the most electronic rubbish.
- ☐ the United States
- ☐ Europe
- ☐ China
- ☐ Germany

g) Another problem is that
- ☐ a lot of e-waste is not recycled properly.
- ☐ only 33 % of e-waste is recycled.
- ☐ millions of phones were collected and recycled.
- ☐ millions of phones were collected in Latin America.

h) In 2016,
- ☐ 12 million new mobile phones were sold.
- ☐ 12 million new mobile phones were bought in the US.
- ☐ 120 million mobile phones were recycled in the US.
- ☐ 120 million mobile phones were sold in the US.

i) Phones and other electronic devices
- ☐ are becoming less complicated.
- ☐ contain precious metals such as gold.
- ☐ have circuit boards made of lithium.
- ☐ have silver coatings.

k) If we do not change our habits,
- ☐ some materials needed for electronic devices will boom.
- ☐ there will be a shortage of electronic inventions.
- ☐ there will be a shortage of rare-earth elements.
- ☐ there will be no rare-earth elements left.

3. The lifeboat clique

Denver Reynolds is an unpopular girl at a high school in Los Angeles (LA) in California. In the following excerpt, she talks about her life at school.

1 My name is Denver Reynolds, Assassin of Dreams, Killer of Friendships. [...]

I moved to LA four years ago, when I was twelve, and I hated it from the start. The myth is that LA can create you, turn you into everything you ever thought you could be. Fill you up with that kind of sparkle that makes for huge houses and adoring crowds. But the truth is,
5 LA can turn on you if you're not on your guard. [...]

The morning [...] started like it always did, just me trying to sleepwalk through high school. Because that is what you do. You sleepwalk. You have a role and a place and a mark on your head that designates your rank. You are certain, when you walk through those doors, who will talk to you and who will not. [...] You know if you are the hunter or the prey. You
10 know if people think you're smart or funny or pretty or geeky or annoying or cool or – worst of all – if they don't think anything about you. Everyone is neatly separated, like a stamp collection. [...] And if I sound bitter, that's because I was. A bitter little stamp left off the envelope of life. But no matter what, I was determined to survive high school. I, Denver Reynolds, would survive.

15 At lunchtime, in the cafeteria, I received my first surprise of the day. I got The Look. An unmistakable moment that led to an unmistakable night and insured that I was in the absolute wrong place at the wrong time.

I'd given up on high school. Given up on anyone trying to understand me or like me or see my value. [...] But at that moment, The Look gave me hope.

20 Our high school lunchroom was set out in an orderly grid. If you Google-Earthed it and zoomed in from above using the satellite setting, you would find that the students were carefully designated by tables. The geek table, the loser table, the student council table, the deeply committed Christian table, the drama table, [...] the rising young felon[1] table (from which oily-looking, detention-bound shoplifters and fire starters glared balefully[2]), and several un-
25 categorized tables, where I sat with various other students who didn't really fit into a group and who ate their lunch fast. There were, in addition, half a dozen tables of ascending social importance that led to that hallowed table in the center of the cafeteria where the most popular kids sat.

It had room for sixteen, and those sixteen had the shiniest teeth, the best hair, the fastest cars,
30 and the sleekest abs[3] in the eleventh grade. The table almost glowed with promise. We, the non-sixteen, couldn't help staring at it. And there, right in the middle of that shining table, was [...] Abigail Kenner. She sat among them, ruling them, passing notes down the table, planning her stupid parties, and laughing her braying[4] laugh that swept over the room, reminding the rest of us that she was in and we were out.

Kathy Parks: The lifeboat clique, Katherine Tegen Books 2016, p. 6–10.

1 felon = criminal
2 balefully = angrily
3 abs = stomach muscles
4 braying = the noise a donkey makes

Answer the questions.

a) What does Denver really think about LA? 1 pt.

b) In Denver's opinion, what is the worst people could think about another student? 1 pt.

c) What does the high school's lunchroom look like? 1 pt.

d) Name two different groups that can be found in the school lunchroom. 2 pts.

e) Where is Denver's place in the school lunchroom? 1 pt.

f) Name two characteristics of the students who sit in the middle of the cafeteria. 2 pts.

You cannot find the answers to the following questions directly in the text:

g) What does Denver mean when she talks about "sleepwalking" through high school? 1 pt.

h) What are Denver's feelings towards Abigail Kenner? 1 pt.

C Use of Language

1. Mediation

Traditional festivities

13 pts.

Jake, ein schottischer Austauschschüler, steht vor einem Plakat am Rathaus. Da er nicht so gut Deutsch spricht, versteht er wenig davon und fragt einen Passanten, was darauf steht. Der Passant wiederum spricht leider nicht so gut Englisch und du bietest deine Hilfe an.

Vermittle zwischen Jake und dem Passanten. Ergänze den folgenden Dialog mit den wichtigsten Informationen in der jeweils geforderten Sprache.

Jake: I keep seeing this poster for a "Hutzelfeuer". What is that?

Du [Deutsch]: _____ 1 pt.

_____

Passant: Ach, das Plakat. Das sieht sehr schön aus, nicht wahr? Beim „Hutzelfeuer" werden die alten Weihnachtsbäume verbrannt. Das Feuer soll den Winter vertreiben. „Hutzelfeuer" ist echt ein komisches Wort. Ich weiß nicht, wo es herkommt.

Du [Englisch]: _____ 2 pts.

_____

_____

Jake: Oh, I see. That sounds fun. What a nice way to end a season! What other customs do you have here?

Du [Deutsch]: _____ 1 pt.

_____

Passant: Lass mich mal überlegen. Das größte Ereignis hier bei uns ist die „Kirmes". Da bauen wir ein Zelt auf und abends spielen Bands. Das ganze Dorf kommt zusammen und wir freuen uns schon das ganze Jahr darauf! Letztes Jahr war ich mit meiner gesamten Familie dort, obwohl es ganz schön kalt war.

Du [Englisch]: _____ 2 pts.

_____

_____

Jake: That sounds like great fun.

Passant: Falls er dann noch hier sein sollte, muss er unbedingt hingehen. Das wird ihm gefallen. Gibt es etwas Ähnliches da, wo er herkommt?

Du [Englisch]: _____ 1 pt.

Jake: I don't think so, but "Burns Night" is very important where I come from. This is a celebration in honour of the Scottish poet Robert Burns. He's probably the most well-known poet of Scotland. "Burns Night" is celebrated at the end of January every year.

Du [Deutsch]: _____ 2 pts.

Passant: Das finde ich sehr ungewöhnlich. Was passiert denn an „Burns Night"? Komisch, dass ich noch nie davon gehört habe, wenn das in Schottland so eine große Sache ist.

Du [Englisch]: _____ 1 pt.

Jake: We always eat "haggis", mashed potato and turnips. Then there are speeches and whisky and people recite poems by Burns. I was sorry to miss it this year. My brother told me all about it.

Du [Deutsch]: _____ 3 pts.

Passant: Das hört sich richtig interessant an. Danke für das Gespräch!

2. Words and structures

Read the text, then tick (✓) the correct words. 12 pts.

Coral reefs in danger

The world's coral reefs, from the Great Barrier Reef in Australia to the Seychelles in the Indian Ocean, are in serious danger __1__ dying out completely by the mid-century unless carbon emissions are reduced enough to slow ocean warming, a new UNESCO study says. And consequences could be severe for millions of __2__.

For a long time, the decline of coral reefs __3__ well documented. But the new study is the first global examination of the entire planet's reef systems, and it __4__ an especially grim picture.

"These are spectacular places, many of __5__ I've visited. Seeing the damage has just been heartbreaking," says Mark Eakin, a reef expert and a lead author of the new report. "We're at the point now where action is essential. It's __6__."

In the next one hundred years, most reef systems will die, unless carbon emissions are reduced. Many others will be gone even __7__.

Reefs, often referred to as the rainforests of the oceans, occupy less than one percent of the ocean floor, but provide habitat for a million species, _8_ a fourth of the world's fish. They also _9_ coastlines against erosion from tropical storms and act as a barrier against rising sea levels.

"It is terrifying to think of the _10_ of the global and large scale loss of reefs," says Ruth Gates, director of the Hawaii Institute of Marine Biology. "The reduction in food supplies, the lack of coastal protection as the reef collapses and subsequent land erosion will make some _11_ unliveable and people will have to move. And that's not even mentioning the collapse of reef-related tourism."

Scientists hope that due to their alarming studies, the world's nations will realize that if they _12_ faster to reduce greenhouse gas emissions, these special places and the people who rely on them will suffer greatly, far sooner than expected.

https://news.nationalgeographic.com/2017/06/coral-reef-bleaching-global-warming-unesco-sites/

1. ☐ for ☐ of ☐ from ☐ off	2. ☐ people ☐ peoples ☐ people's ☐ peoples'	3. ☐ is ☐ was ☐ has been ☐ had been	4. ☐ takes ☐ paints ☐ brushes ☐ pictures
5. ☐ which ☐ who ☐ what ☐ where	6. ☐ upset ☐ urgent ☐ unless ☐ urban	7. ☐ later ☐ further ☐ sooner ☐ afterwards	8. ☐ adding ☐ including ☐ incorporating ☐ excluding
9. ☐ protected ☐ protection ☐ protecting ☐ protect	10. ☐ effects ☐ conclusions ☐ meanings ☐ impressions	11. ☐ situations ☐ positions ☐ country ☐ places	12. ☐ won't act ☐ didn't act ☐ don't act ☐ hadn't acted

D Text Production

*Choose one of the following tasks and write about 150 words.
Count your words and write the number at the end of the text.*

25 pts.

What is the story behind the picture?

Imagine this photo is the object of a creative writing competition and you decide to enter.

Write a text and include at least **four** of the following aspects:
- Who are the people?
- Where are they?
- What is happening?
- How do they feel?
- What will happen next?

or

A good night's sleep

You have noticed that lots of students don't get enough sleep. So you decide to write an article for your English school magazine about sleeping habits.
Use the ideas below to state your opinion.

Include at least **four** of the following aspects:
- Do you have problems sleeping/falling asleep?
- What are your sleeping habits like?
- Is getting a good night's sleep important or just a waste of time?
- Why do teenagers go to bed so late in the evening?
- How does sleep affect success in school?

**Hessen Realschule – Englisch
Jahrgang 2019**

Listening Comprehension – Transcripts

Hello, this is the listening exam. I am going to give you the instructions for the test. There are three parts to the listening exam. At the beginning of each part, you'll hear this sound: ◀
You may write down your answers at any point during the listening exam.

Part One

In part one you will hear two news items. You will hear the news items twice. Before listening to each news item, you will have 20 seconds to read the tasks. You now have 20 seconds to read the tasks for news item one. *(20 seconds break)* You are now going to hear the first news item for the first time. After a short break, you will hear the news item again. ◀

News Item 1: 10,000 Year Clock

Deep inside a mountain along the Texas-Mexico border stands a 60-metre tall clock that ticks just once a year. It also has a clock hand that moves once every one hundred years, and a cuckoo which will appear once every 1,000 years. This is the 10,000 Year Clock!
Although inventor Danny Hillis first had the idea in 1995, it was not until 2011, when American CEO Jeff Bezos agreed to finance the project, that work on a full-scale version of the 10,000 Year Clock began properly. The clock is still under construction and will cost approximately $42 million. It is housed in a 150-metre tall tunnel inside a mountain owned by the billionaire.
It is made of tough, long-lasting materials, like titanium, ceramic and stone and works with the help of giant gears and dials. Its power comes from thermal energy captured by changes in day and nighttime temperatures on the mountain top.
The timepiece's bells will ring ten times a day, playing unique melodies that will never be repeated over the 10,000 years. Bezos says he hopes the clock will "change the way humanity thinks about time and encourage people to take a longer view of things." It turns out Bezos is not the only one who thinks the 10,000 Year Clock is a brilliant way of connecting with future generations. A second one is already being planned inside a mountain in eastern Nevada.

Adapted from: https://www.dogonews.com/2018/3/31/massive-clock-buried-under-texas-mountain-top-will-keep-ticking-for-10000-years (last accessed on 01. 05. 2018).

You now have 20 seconds to read the tasks for news item two. *(20 seconds break)* You are now going to hear the second news item for the first time. After a short break, you will hear news item two again. ◀

News Item 2: Pies on π-Day

Everybody knows that pi is the number 3.14, and that you need this number to calculate, for example, the surface area of a circle, but did you know that in America, there is a special day celebrating this mathematical phenomenon?
Pi Day is on March the 14th, which also happens to be Albert Einstein's birthday. Students at the California Institute of Technology in Los Angeles celebrate Pi Day by holding a pie-eating contest, which begins at 1:59 am and features 26 pies, with five different flavors. This might seem a bit strange, but put all the numbers together – 3.14 (the date), 159 (the time), 26 (the number of pies) and 5 (the flavors) – and you have the first nine digits of pi: 3.14159265!
Princeton University in New Jersey, on the other hand, where Einstein lived from 1935 until his death in 1955, celebrates Pi Day with many festi-

vities. Visitors can go to concerts and shows, eat fruit pies and even take part in an Einstein lookalike contest.

Although the celebration is just 25 years old, the number itself is almost 4,000 years old. The Babylonians first calculated pi to a value of three, and the ancient Egyptians calculated pi as 3.165 in 1650 BC. It was the Greeks, however, who first worked out pi accurately in the third century BC. If you remember that this number was discovered without the help of computers, their results are truly amazing! Happy Pi Day!

Adapted from: https://www.dogonews.com/2018/3/13/prepare-to-celebrate-your-math-skills-and-sweet-tooth-on-pi-e-day (last accessed on 25. 03. 2018).

Part Two

> In part two a reporter is carrying out a survey. You will hear this twice. Before listening, you will have 40 seconds to read the task. You now have 40 seconds to read the task. *(40 seconds break)*
> You are now going to hear the survey for the first time. After a short break, you will hear the survey again. ◀

Survey: Summer holidays

Reporter: Hello everybody! What is the ideal holiday for teenagers? Some teens want to hang around the pool, while others like to explore the world. This morning, I talked to some teenagers in Greenwich and I asked them about their ideas for a perfect holiday. Here are their opinions:

Rosie: My name is Rosie. Holidays on the beach are boring, so last year I went to a summer camp for international students in Alicante in Spain. I enjoyed learning Spanish and I made lots of new friends. The programme also had a great mix of cultural, sporting and leisure activities.

David: Hello, my name is David. Last year I went to Spain with my parents. We stayed in an amazing hotel and I met loads of nice people and had a fantastic time! But my parents …! In the evenings, I had to be back in my room by 10 pm. I was so angry about that, so we often quarrelled with each other. They worry far too much, even on holiday.

Jessica: Hi, I'm Jessica. Last summer I went to the island of Corfu with some friends. Our hotel was in Kavos and the city really comes alive at night. There are discos and great bars full of young people. I didn't get much of a suntan, but it was definitely the highlight of the year for me.

Dean: My name is Dean. I prefer holidays with my friends too. We all love surfing and St. Ives in Cornwall is just perfect for improving your boarding skills. If you don't feel like surfing, however, there is plenty of other stuff to do, for example kayaking and stand-up paddling or simply just chilling out at a beach café. It's ideal.

Kendra: Hello everyone! I'm Kendra. The last time I went on holiday with my parents, my mum kept borrowing my clothes and my dad acted as if he was 19. I was so annoyed with them. This year, I'm going to Rimini in Italy with a group of friends. That will be much better.

Mark: Hi everybody! My name's Mark. I love family holidays. We often go hiking and cycling in Snowdon National Park in Wales. The views from the top of Mount Snowdon are amazing. It might not be everybody's cup of tea, though. There's nowhere to plug in your phone, so that might be a problem for some people.

Emily: Hi. I'm Emily. Next year I want to work abroad. This will give me the chance of earning some money over the summer before I go back to university in September. Working abroad also gives you the feeling of being on holiday, and I like that too.

Reporter: Thank you for all your interesting comments.

Part Three

In part three you will hear an interview. You will hear the interview twice. Before listening to the interview, you will have 30 seconds to read the task. You now have 30 seconds to read the task.
(30 seconds break) You are now going to hear the interview for the first time. After a short break, you will hear the interview again. ◀

Interview: Katie McDonnell

Reporter: Our guest this morning is freerunner Katie McDonnell. Good morning, Katie. Thank you for coming in today.

Katie: Hi, thanks for having me.

Reporter: Katie, you're a freerunner, otherwise known as a professional parkour athlete. Could you please tell our listeners what freerunning is? I'm not sure they all know.

Katie: Well, freerunning is basically moving in open spaces. This involves running, climbing, swinging and jumping and it's normally done in built-up areas.

Reporter: Right, I see. And how did you get into this sport?

Katie: It all started while I was at university. I was in my first year and I was looking for a new hobby, so I started cheerleading in my free time. I went along to gym sessions and that's where I met a group of guys who did freerunning. They showed me a few moves and gradually I found that I was spending more time training for freerunning than for cheerleading.

Reporter: And when did you realize you could make a living by leaping off buildings?

Katie: I was in my final year at university and I was offered a few commercial jobs. When I realized that there was actually potential for me to do this as a career, I started thinking, "Wow, I really am going to have a go at this."

Reporter: And it has worked out great, hasn't it? Let us talk about the type of work you have done. You have taken part in advertising campaigns and in films. You have also been on TV and performed live.

Katie: Yes, the last six years really have been amazing. I have done stunts for various actresses as well. For example, I doubled Milla Jovovich in the film "Resident Evil", I had to complete a parkour sequence in a laser beam tunnel. The most exciting thing about my job, however, is that it allows me to travel so much. I've been on film location in Venice, Barcelona, Rome, LA, Buenos Aires, all over the world.

Reporter: You make it look so simple. How much training do you do?

Katie: A lot! I work hard in the gym as well as on the streets. I need to keep my body in shape, so I do an hour or two most evenings, doing pull-ups and 10 kg weights, as well as running for fitness and leg strength. I try to train in a way that will increase my explosivity, that's really important in parkour.

Reporter: Well, you look great, Katie, if I may say so! Katie, you have over 160,000 followers online and this has helped make freerunning more and more popular. How can people get involved in this sport?

Katie: I would look for classes online. If you want to get into parkour properly though, you should try and find out whether there is a parkour community near where you live. Training with other people who have more experience is a great way to learn and progress. There are loads of tutorials online to help you get started.

Reporter: Thanks for the tip! What do you like best about freerunning?

Katie: What I love about this sport is that there are no limitations, no rules. You can train anywhere, in the city, in the jungle or in the forest. It's all down to your own creativity.

Reporter: Thank you for joining us on the show today, Katie.

Adapted from: http://www.bbc.co.uk/bbcthree/clip/50efdfdf-ee35-4494-8e1b-b147b0ffcd8c (last accessed on 08.03.2018), http://metro.co.uk/2015/10/01/incredible-freerunner-reveals-the-secret-to-her-rock-hard-abs-5404346/ (last accessed on 08.03.2018).

You may now continue with the rest of the exam. Good luck!

Abschlussprüfung Englisch 2019

A Listening Comprehension

Part One

Listen to the news items and tick (✓) the right statements.
There is only one possible answer per statement.

News Item 1: 10,000 Year Clock
4 pts.

a) The clock hand moves once every
- [ ] year.
- [ ] one hundred years.
- [ ] one thousand years.

b) Work on the clock started in
- [ ] 1995.
- [ ] 2000.
- [ ] 2011.

c) The clock gets its power from
- [ ] changes in temperature.
- [ ] giant gears and dials.
- [ ] solar energy.

d) Jeff Bezos hopes the clock will
- [ ] connect with future generations of clocks.
- [ ] change how we think about time.
- [ ] never be repeated.

News Item 2: Pies on π-Day
4 pts.

a) Pi Day celebrates
- [ ] the scientist Albert Einstein.
- [ ] delicious American pies.
- [ ] a famous number.

b) In Los Angeles, the pie-eating competition begins
- [ ] in the afternoon.
- [ ] in the evening.
- [ ] at night.

c) On Pi Day in Princeton, you can
- [ ] practice your math.
- [ ] dress up as Albert Einstein.
- [ ] make pies.

d) Pi was first calculated accurately by the
- [ ] Greeks.
- [ ] Egyptians.
- [ ] Babylonians.

Part Two

Survey: Summer holidays

Listen to these people talking about summer holidays.
Who thinks what? Write the correct letters in the chart.
Be careful – there is one statement more than you need.

7 pts.

A I want to do water sports and relax with friends.

B My parents always want to keep a close eye on me. That's annoying.

C Going on a nature holiday with the family is wonderful.

D I like learning a foreign language and meeting new people.

E Some parents behave on holiday as if they were still teenagers.

F It's important to make summer holidays a family decision.

G If you want to do something different, try a working holiday.

H A holiday with friends on a party island is the best.

Rosie	David	Jessica	Dean	Kendra	Mark	Emily

Part Three

Interview: Katie McDonnell

Listen to the interview and write down the information needed.
Fill in only one detail per box.

10 pts.

where she found out about freerunning	
what sport she did before freerunning	
types of work (2 details)	
most exciting thing about her job	
training (2 details)	
number of Internet followers	
how you can get involved in freerunning	
what she loves about the sport	

B Reading Comprehension

1. Somalia's team on ice

❶ Sweden, now home to more than 200,000 refugees and asylum seekers, once called itself a "humanitarian superpower" with an open door policy for new arrivals. Yet the rising number of refugees has worsened tensions across the country. Somalis living in Sweden are experiencing increased hostility as the political climate changes against migrants. Some new arrivals have been forced to live in camps, others have experienced death threats and arson attacks.

❷ Hans Grandin was nearing retirement when he realized he wanted to do something to change the social structure of his town Borlänge. It is around 200 km north of Stockholm and home to more than 3,000 Somalis. "Integration is not, was not, as good as it can be. It takes a long time, especially in Sweden, where people are cold and slow," he says. "There was already a refugee football team, and I thought we could do something similar, helping the Somalis get on ice." So the idea was that they should play bandy, a version of ice hockey played with a ball.

❸ Bandy originated in the UK in the 19th century before spreading to Scandinavia and the USSR[1], who set up the Federation of International Bandy in 1955. In fact, it is still very popular in Sweden and Russia today. "Bandy is similar to football, the rules, positions and the gameplay, but the hardest thing is to be able to skate quickly and manage the stick," explains Mohammed Ahmmed, a Somali player, 19 years old. Most of Somalia's bandy team had never seen snow or ice before they arrived in Sweden as refugees in their late teens.

❹ After helping to establish the team, Grandin met film-maker Patrick Andersson, who had the idea to register Somalia with the International Bandy Federation, and things accelerated. Soon after, they entered the 2014 world championships and found themselves with just six months to assemble a strong group of worthy players. "We hold the record for the world's worst team ever to play in the championship," says Grandin. But although they didn't find sporting success last year, they certainly caused a sensation in Sweden's media.

❺ The team's chairman, Mursal Ismail, a 34-year-old who has lived in Sweden since 2002, said it's an important way "for Somalis to show themselves doing good things for their host country." He admits that he has faced "some hostilities" but maintains that "the majority of the people are very welcoming". Though the players talk of being under a lot of pressure and are training hard, Ismail says it is not just about the sport. It is also about trying to "make integration work". For Grandin, the success of the project will be shown in how "political language changes and how people's hearts change."

https://www.theguardian.com/world/2016/jan/04/the-cool-runnings-of-the-refugee-crisis-somalias-bandy-team-at-home-on-ice

1 USSR = abbreviation for the Union of Soviet Socialist Republics (1922–1991)

Match the five correct headings to each part of the text (1–5).
Be careful – there are two headings more than you need. 5 pts.

A	A FAST GAME ON ICE
B	MORE THAN SPORT
C	RESEARCH ON INTEGRATION
D	A NEW IDEA FOR INTEGRATION
E	RISING PROBLEMS
F	TRYING TO KEEP PEOPLE OUT
G	GETTING WORLDWIDE ATTENTION

part of the text	❶	❷	❸	❹	❺
heading					

2. The story of circus

In honour of the 250th anniversary of the circus, we decided to put together a brief history of circus milestones.

In 1768, Philip Astley, a former cavalry officer, opened an equestrian[1] school in London, giving riding lessons in the morning and performing trick riding stunts in the afternoon. Performances took place in a circular ring but it was not called a circus. Within two years, acrobats and clowning were part of the mix.

The first structure to be called a circus, however, was the Royal Circus, built in 1782 in south London by Astley's rival, Charles Hughes. Acts included horsemanship, tightrope walking, trampoline and tumbling acts. A decade later, the Scotsman John Bill Ricketts opened the US's first circus in 1793, with President George Washington as one of the early attendees.

It was in 1825, though, that Joshua Purdy Brown erected the first circus tent in Wilmington, Delaware. It was a year before the first circular tent – which, together with the sawdust[2] ring, became so associated with travelling circuses in Europe and America. The tent was one of the most important features in allowing circus to develop, reach new audiences and do shows regardless of rain or storm.

Jules Léotard gave the first public performance of an aerial[3] trapeze act in 1859, which he developed by hanging swings above his father's swimming pool in Toulouse. The water broke his frequent falls during training. During public performances, he used mattresses or no protection at all because the safety net was not invented until 1871. Léotard also gave his name to the one-piece costume.

Fourteen-year-old Rossa Matilda Richter, who performed under the stage name Zazel, was the first recorded person to be launched out of a cannon. It launched her more than six metres before she landed in a net in a performance at the Royal Aquarium in 1877. She continued to perform her act for another 14 years, until her career was ended when she was shot from a cannon in New Mexico, the net failed and she got hurt.

Love them or hate them, clowns – descendants of the jester[4] figure, which dates back to the times of knights and kings – are an essential part of circus shows. Right from its start, clowns began entertaining audiences and are still a feature of traditional circuses. In the UK, the most prominent was Coco the Clown, who was born Nicolai Poliakoff in Latvia in 1900.

The arrival of railways in the 1830s had a huge influence on circus: now companies could travel widely with ease. PT Barnum had a train to transport 1,000 staff members, 30 elephants and a big top[5]. Without the railways, circus would never have become such a popular entertainment in the US.

Canadian troupe Cirque du Soleil was founded in Montreal in 1984. Its modern, dazzling, high-quality acts with theatrical elements have come a long way from the simplicity of the sawdust ring. It is now serious professional entertainment.

In the USA, the Ringling Brothers Circus, the "Greatest Show on Earth", gave its last performance in 2017 after 146 years on the road, claiming there had been a sharp drop in ticket sales after the company stopped using elephants. The use of wild animals in performance is in fact banned in some countries today.

https://www.theguardian.com/stage/2018/jan/19/chainsaw-juggling-human-cannonballs-and-coco-the-clown-the-astounding-250-year-story-of-circus

1 equestrian = *here:* connected with riding horses
2 sawdust = powder that falls when wood is cut
3 aerial = in the air
4 jester = professional joker or "fool"
5 big top = large circus tent

Tick (✓) the right statement. There is only one possible answer per statement. 10 pts.

a) Philip Astley's performances included
- [ ] trapeze acts, acrobats and riding stunts.
- [ ] horse-riding, acrobats and clowns.
- [ ] tightrope walking, clowns and tumbling.
- [ ] horse-riding, human cannon balls and trampolines.

b) The name "circus" was first used in
- [ ] 1768.
- [ ] 1782.
- [ ] 1793.
- [ ] 1825.

c) The first circus tent was built by
   ☐ Charles Hughes.
   ☐ John Bill Rickets.
   ☐ Joshua Purdy Brown.
   ☐ Philip Astley.

d) The use of tents enabled circuses to
   ☐ develop trapeze acts.
   ☐ associate with European circuses.
   ☐ perform in a sawdust ring.
   ☐ perform in all weathers.

e) Jules Léotard trained using
   ☐ thick mattresses.
   ☐ no protection at all.
   ☐ the safety net.
   ☐ his father's pool.

f) Zazel, the first human cannonball, performed her act until
   ☐ she was shot in Mexico.
   ☐ she missed the safety net.
   ☐ the cannon failed.
   ☐ she had an accident.

g) Clowns have been part of the circus since
   ☐ its beginning.
   ☐ 1830.
   ☐ 1900.
   ☐ 1984.

h) Circuses gained in popularity after the introduction of
   ☐ the safety net.
   ☐ train tracks.
   ☐ elephants.
   ☐ the big top.

i) Since 1984, elements of modern circus have often included
   ☐ wild animals.
   ☐ a sawdust ring.
   ☐ theatre.
   ☐ clowns.

k) Many people stopped going to the circus because
- [ ] the ticket prices went up.
- [ ] of a new wild animal act.
- [ ] they couldn't see elephants anymore.
- [ ] the Ringling Brothers gave their last performance.

3. Winter classroom

Fourteen-year-old Madeline lives with her parents in the beautiful wild woods of northern Minnesota (USA). The area where they live is rather isolated and she is an outsider at school. In the following extract, she is sitting in class.

1 PAPERS PASSED ALONG IN A PILE. That's what high school was. They went down one aisle between desks, came back around the next, looped slowly to the back of the classroom. The gifted and talented kids [...] licked their fingers to extract their portion. They always set to work like the swim team doing laps, breathing from the sides of their mouths, biting down
5 on their pencils. The hockey players had to be prodded awake when the stack came down their aisle, had to be treated with great deference[1] – or else we would lose the District Championship. Again. They woke from their naps long enough to take one paper and pass the rest on, long enough to dump open bags of chips into their mouths, wipe the salt from their lips, and return to their dreams of Empire. What else would hockey players dream about?

10 It was their world we lived in. When I was fifteen, I figured this out. They dreamed it into fact. They got teachers to forgive their blank worksheets, they got cheerleaders to scream out their names at pep rallies[2] [...]. We were in a new building that year, a bigger classroom with pale brick walls, but outside it was the same thing it had been since we were children. Winter boomeranged back.

15 Outside: four feet of snow sealed in a shiny crust.

Inside: European History, American Civics, Trigonometry, English.

Life Science[3] came last. It was taught by our old eighth-grade gym teacher, Liz Lundgren, who trudged over from the middle school at the end of the day in her Polartec parka and camouflage snow bib[4]. Ms. Lundgren had a tic. Whenever she got irritated or inspired, she
20 switched instantly to whispering. She thought that would make us listen better; she thought it would make us pay attention to protists and fungi[5]; she thought we would try harder to understand meiosis if we couldn't quite catch all the words in her sentences. "The spores ... in absence of water or heat ... maneuver in great quantities," she would murmur, and it was like hearing some obscure rumor that, due to over-telling, no longer held any relevance we
25 could make out.

In that class you could always hear the clock tick. From every window, you could see snow blow away in gusts, then drift back the next day in piles as high as houses. One day near the end of Evolution, a late-season storm brought a huge poplar branch down in a wumff of ice. Through the window, I watched it cascade to the ground and narrowly miss a small blue car
30 pulling out from the grocery store across from school. At the board, Ms. Lundgren was

chalking out the pros and cons of natural selection in squeaky cursive. The window fogged as I leaned toward it. I leaned back. Someone in a huge hooded parka got out of the blue car, dragged the branch from the road, got back in. Then the Honda drove a wide arc around the perimeter, crunching a few twigs beneath its tires.

35 Minutes after that the sun came out: brilliant, stunning us all. Still, it was no surprise when we were let out of school a half hour early due to the windchill.

Emily Fridlund: History of Wolves. London: Weidenfeld & Nicolson 2007, S. 20–22, adaptiert

1 deference = respect
2 pep rally = a motivational speech
3 Life Science (US) = Biology
4 snow bib = snow trousers
5 protists and fungi = simple biological organisms

Answer the questions.

a) Which two different groups of students can be found in the classroom? (two details)   2 pts.

b) Name two examples which show that some students are not interested in learning.   2 pts.

c) Why does Ms. Lundgren start whispering when she gets irritated or inspired?   1 pt.

d) How does Madeline feel about Life Science?   1 pt.

e) What are winters in Minnesota like? (two details)   2 pts.

You cannot find the answers to the following questions directly in the text:

f) Why do the teachers forgive the hockey players for handing in blank worksheets?   1 pt.

g) Why does Madeline watch the scene outside the window so intently? 1 pt.

C Use of Language

1. **Mediation** 13 pts.

   Volunteer work

   Du bist mit Tiffany, einer Verwandten aus den USA, im Urlaub an der Nordsee. Ihr besucht die Insel Wangerooge und nehmt an einer geführten Wanderung teil. Eure Führerin ist Claudia, die auf der Insel ein Freiwilliges Ökologisches Jahr macht. Tiffany möchte mehr darüber erfahren.

   Vermittle zwischen Tiffany und Claudia. Ergänze den folgenden Dialog mit den wichtigsten Informationen in der jeweils geforderten Sprache.

   Tiffany: I understand that Claudia is doing some volunteer work here on the island. Could you ask her what kind of volunteer work that is?

   Du [Deutsch]: _____ 1 pt.

   Claudia: Ich mache ein sogenanntes Freiwilliges Ökologisches Jahr. Nach der Schule wusste ich nicht genau, was ich weiter machen sollte – da habe ich schon erst mal in der Luft gehangen. Aber da ich mich schon immer für Naturschutz interessiert hatte, dachte ich, das Freiwillige Ökologische Jahr wäre die perfekte Sache für mich.

   Du [Englisch]: _____ 2 pts.

   Tiffany: Oh, that sounds interesting. Especially in such a beautiful place! What are her tasks here on the island?

   Du [Deutsch]: _____ 1 pt.

   Claudia: Hauptsächlich mache ich Führungen. Besonders mag ich die Besuche von Schulklassen, denn die Kinder sind immer so begeistert! Manchmal muss ich auch noch Büro- und Gartenarbeiten machen. Das macht mir nicht immer so viel Spaß, muss aber auch sein … man kann ja nicht alles haben.

   Du [Englisch]: _____ 2 pts.

Tiffany:	Wow, that's truly impressive. What has been the most exciting thing that has happened to her so far?	
Du [Deutsch]:	Was ist das spannenste was dir passiert ist	1 pt.
Claudia:	Das war vor zwei Wochen, als Touristen ein verlassenes Seehundbaby am Strand meldeten. Ich schnappte mir sofort das Fernglas und rannte los, um das zu überprüfen. Zum Glück war es ein falscher Alarm und die Mutter holte das Kleine ab.	
Du [Englisch]:	_____	2 pts.
Tiffany:	Wow, that sounds really exciting. We saw some of them today. They are so cute.	
Claudia:	Tiffany wirkt so überrascht. Gibt es so etwas Ähnliches nicht auch in Amerika?	
Du [Englisch]:	_____	1 pt.
Tiffany:	Not exactly. But we do have the "Peace Corps", where you can volunteer for projects around the world. Last year, a friend of mine went to Tanzania, a country in Africa, to build water tanks. What she told me about that experience really impressed me.	
Du [Deutsch]:	_____	2 pts.
Claudia:	Das hört sich aber auch spannend an! Ich bin froh, dass ich euch getroffen habe. Lasst uns doch unsere Nummern austauschen und in Kontakt bleiben.	
Du [Englisch]:	_____	1 pt.
Tiffany:	Great idea! Here is my number! I'll give her my e-mail address too!	

2. Words and structures

Read the text, then tick (✓) the correct words. 12 pts.

Getting kids interested in chemistry

Can you imagine a teacher who breathes fire and makes explosions? Kate Biberdorf is no imaginary teacher. A lecturer from Texas, she describes __1__ as a kid at heart. "I love explosions, mixing things up and seeing what will happen," she says. "I'm always messy and dirty. I __2__ love my job."

That job involves __3__ thousands of students chemistry every year. Her goal is to show kids that chemistry is exciting and that __4__ can become a chemist. Through her hands-on approach to teaching, Biberdorf is breaking down the image of the stereotypical scientist.

She is also reaching students that otherwise __5__ intimidated by science and hopes to host an explosive science show in Las Vegas one day.

__6__ does she love chemistry so much? Because she says it "explains everything in life," including computers and flowers, how clocks work, why cement __7__ from liquid to solid, what happens when you breathe, your emotions and even why you sweat. Biberdorf also loves teaching her students about the science of healthy living and encourages them to exercise, eat __8__ and drink more water. If she wasn't a chemist, she says, she __9__ a fitness instructor, someone who actually helps others to find a better and healthier lifestyle.

Students' emotional responses, rather than pure memorization of facts, is key to Biberdorf's way of teaching, as well as science in general. She has an important piece of advice for kids who are interested in __10__ with subjects like chemistry, biology or physics and perhaps becoming a scientist one day. Especially in math and science, she recommends studying hard __11__ school.

"The best thing to do is to ask why," she says. "If you're always asking questions, you're __12__ a scientist."

https://www.washingtonpost.com/lifestyle/kidspost/this-teacher-aims-to-get-kids-fired-up-about-chemistry/2018/03/26/c99e7bf6-225f-11e8-badd-7c9f29a55815_story.html?utm_term=.a57889933644 (abgerufen am 10. 05. 2018, adaptiert).
https://www.katethechemist.com/bio (abgerufen am 07. 06. 2018, adaptiert).

1. ☒ herself ☐ her ☐ she ☐ hers	2. ☐ easily ☐ easy ☒ simply ☐ simple	3. ☒ teaching ☐ taught ☐ going to teach ☐ will teach	4. ☐ somebody ☒ anyone ☐ anything ☐ someone
5. ☒ might be ☐ have to be ☐ are able to ☐ might	6. ☐ Where ☐ How ☐ What ☒ Why	7. ☐ becomes ☐ mixes ☒ turns ☐ stays	8. ☐ healthiest ☐ healthily ☐ health ☒ healthy
9. ☐ has been ☐ will be ☐ had been ☒ would be	10. ☒ having fun ☐ being funny ☐ have fun ☐ be funny	11. ☐ by ☐ on ☒ at ☐ of	12. ☒ already ☐ still ☐ ever ☐ never

D Text Production

Choose one of the following tasks and write about 150 words.
Count your words and write the number at the end of the text.   25 pts.

What is the story behind the picture?

Imagine this photo is the object of a writing competition and you decide to enter.

Write a text and include at least four of the following aspects:
- Who is the boy?
- Why is he there?
- What happened before?
- Why is the cat with him?
- What will happen next?

https://animalstalkinginallcaps.tumblr.com

or

Glamour and Glory

Your school had a competition on the coolest classroom and your class has won the first prize of 100 Euros.

Write a report for your English school magazine and include at least four of the following aspects:
- What did you do to improve your classroom?
- What motivated your classmates to get involved?
- How did you organize the work of your classmates?
- Why was your classroom better than the others?
- What will your class do with the prize money?

Hessen Realschule – Englisch
Jahrgang 2020

Listening Comprehension – Transcripts

Hello, this is the listening exam. I am going to give you the instructions for the test. There are three parts to the listening exam. At the beginning of each part, you'll hear this sound: ◀
You may write down your answers at any point during the listening exam.

Part One

In part one you will hear two news items. You will hear the news items twice. Before listening to each news item, you will have 20 seconds to read the tasks. You now have 20 seconds to read the tasks for news item one. *(20 seconds break)* You are now going to hear the first news item for the first time. After a short break, you will hear the news item again. ◀

News Item 1: Rapunzel

A twelve-year-old girl, who is known in her neighbourhood as Rapunzel, is finally going to have her first haircut next week and plans to sell her hair for around £ 3,500. Natasha Moraes de Andrade, who lives in Rio de Janeiro, Brazil, has never had a haircut. At one metre sixty, she is just two centimetres taller than the length of her beautiful, thick brown hair. Natasha spends four hours per week washing her hair and up to an hour-and-a-half brushing it daily. She has to carry it when she walks and folds it up when she sits down. Despite temperatures of over 40 degrees in Rio, Natasha's family cannot switch on the fan because her hair gets caught in it. The heat in the house is a real problem for them all. Children often stand outside her house and shout "Rapunzel, Rapunzel, let down your hair!" Her life is impossible – she can't do sport in school because her hair gets in the way and, although she lives close to the beach, she can't go swimming because the seawater damages her hair and it takes hours to wash the salt out. With the money for her hair, Natasha wants to redo her bedroom and start a new life as a normal girl.

Deborah Arthurs: Real-life Rapunzel, 12, set to cut hair for the first time … and plans to sell the 5ft 2in mane for £ 3,500, MailOnline vom 20. 03. 2012, https://www.dailymail.co.uk/femail/article-2117592/Natasha-Moraes-Andrade-Real-life-Rapunzel-12-cuts-hair-time.html

You now have 20 seconds to read the tasks for news item two. *(20 seconds break)* You are now going to hear the second news item for the first time. After a short break, you will hear news item two again. ◀

News Item 2: Big Ben marathon runner

A London Marathon runner dressed as Big Ben got stuck at the finish line after he tried to break a world record. Lukas Bates, from Maidstone in Kent, tried to get into the Guinness World Record Book for the fastest time dressed as a landmark. The current record stands at three hours and 34 minutes. Lukas finished with a time of three hours and 54 minutes. However, even with the help of a race volunteer, the 30-year-old was unable to fit under the race clock at the finishing line because the top of his Big Ben costume was too tall. In the end, after two full minutes of trying to cross the line, and with the help of another runner, Lukas finally crossed over the line on his hands and knees.
Speaking after the marathon, Lukas said that he had a personal best time of two hours and 59 minutes – when not dressed as a clock. The record for the fastest marathon time dressed as a landmark, such as a building or a place, was set by Richard Mietz at the Berlin Marathon in September last year, when he ran dressed as the Lübeck Holstentor city gate.

London Marathon: Big Ben runner gets stuck at finish line, BBC vom 28. April 2019, https://www.bbc.co.uk/news/uk-england-london-48084878

Part Two

> In part two a reporter is carrying out a survey. You will hear this twice. Before listening, you will have 40 seconds to read the task. You now have 40 seconds to read the task. *(40 seconds break)*
> You are now going to hear the survey for the first time. After a short break, you will hear the survey again. ◄

Survey: Eating insects

Reporter: Last week I drove past a "pestaurant", a pop-up stand offering dry roasted worms and chocolate covered ants. Is this really the food of the future? Is eating insects really good for you? Last Tuesday, I asked shoppers in Churchill Square shopping centre in Brighton what they knew about this topic. Here is a selection of their answers.

Julie: Hi, my name is Julie. Eating insects may seem like a really disgusting thing for us here in Europe, but it really isn't a new thing. Insects are a regular part of the diet in many countries in Central and South America, Africa and Asia. When we went to Australia, I discovered that the Aborigines have eaten larvae like wichetty grubs for thousands of years.

David: Good morning. I'm David. Even though they look horrible, you may be surprised to learn that insects are really good for you. For example, a 100-gramme portion of red ants contains about 14 grammes of protein as well as a lot of iron. Many other insects are a great source of nutrients as well.

Mia: Good morning, my name is Mia. I read recently that worldwide, farming animals produces up to 18 % of all greenhouse gases produced by human activity, which in turn speeds up global warming. Farming insects, however, produces between 10 and 80 times less methane gas than farming other animals. I think this is good news for all of us.

Archie: Hi, Archie here. I wouldn't eat an insect if you gave me a million pounds! Let's be honest, there are good reasons why we try to keep bugs away from our food instead of eating them. Many insects feed on rotting food, dead animals and human waste, which is full of bacteria, and unfortunately, many insect farms in Asia don't follow high hygienic standards and this results in illness.

Katy: Hi, everyone, my name is Katy. Did you know that insect farms are not as difficult to operate as cattle farms? There is less chance that insects will catch diseases which will cross over to humans and the best thing is that insects are easy to harvest. Even if we don't eat insects ourselves, they could replace the expensive and often environmentally unfriendly products which are fed to chicken and fish which we do eat.

Dora: Morning, I'm Dora. It's funny you've asked me about eating insects. I've just done a project on this topic in school. A kilogramme of feed given to a cricket will produce twelve times more protein than the same amount given to cattle, so this means that the farming of insects requires less water and feed than any other farmed animals.

Jenna: Hi, Jenna here. You might not find the idea of scoffing insects particularly attractive, but we actually already eat more insects than you think. Do you eat any red-coloured foods? Yogurts, juices, sausages? Well that's likely the natural food colouring cochineal, which is so popular, it even has its own E-number, E120. This natural colouring, which is also used in lipsticks and blushes, comes from a small bug found in North and South America.

Reporter: As you can see, there may well be good reasons for eating insects, but not all people are convinced that it is the food of the future. Back to the studio in London.

Adapted from: https://www.youtube.com/watch?v=No7zYX20Ejs (last accessed on 11.05.2019).
https://www.eatcrickster.com/blog/pros-and-cons-of-eating-insects (last accessed on 11.05.2019).

Part Three

> In part three you will hear an interview. You will hear the interview twice. Before listening to the interview, you will have 30 seconds to read the task. You now have 30 seconds to read the task.
> *(30 seconds break)* You are now going to hear the interview for the first time. After a short break, you will hear the interview again. ◀

Interview: Ross Edgley's Great British swim

Reporter: Our guest in the studio today is Ross Edgley who has just become the first person to swim around Great Britain. Thank you for coming in today, Ross.

Ross: Thank you. It's great to be here.

Reporter: Ross, you swam 2,885 kilometres around the coast of Great Britain. That is amazing! First question, Ross – why? Why would anyone want to do that?

Ross: I guess I wasn't made for a nine-to-five job. I think I need the adventure.

Reporter: You have two other world records. You hold the record for the longest rope climb. You climbed 8,800 metres in 19 hours. You have also run a marathon pulling a small car. How did swimming around Great Britain compare to these other challenges?

Ross: Well, it took longer, obviously, and really tested my physical and mental strength.

Reporter: That doesn't surprise me. Let's talk about the swim itself. When and where did you start?

Ross: I left Margate on the south-east coast of England on the 1st of June and arrived back in Margate 157 days later.

Reporter: I read that you were hoping to complete the swim in 100 days. What went wrong?

Ross: Well, the weather was unpredictable. There were days when the waves were really high. There were strong currents and to be honest, the cold slowed me down too.

Reporter: What sort of routine did you have?

Ross: I swam for six hours and then slept for six hours. You have to swim when the tides are right, of course.

Reporter: So at the end of each day you swam back to the shore and slept in a hotel bed and then went out the next day and did the same thing again?

Ross: No, I didn't touch land for 23 weeks. I slept on the support boat. If I had gone into shore, I would not have broken the record for the longest sea swim.

Reporter: There must have been some dark moments when you thought you would not make it.

Ross: Well, all in all I was stung 37 times by jellyfish. I also had open wounds on my body where my wetsuit rubbed me and I damaged the muscles in my shoulder.

Reporter: What did you eat to give you enough energy?

Ross: I ate between 10,000 and 15,000 calories every day, that's up to six times the male average. Pizza, pasta, rice pudding. 610 bananas and 314 cans of energy drinks. I did miss my mum's cheesecake though.

Reporter: And how did it feel when you left the boat for the last swim on the last day?

Ross: I was really emotional. I was accompanied by 300 swimmers for the last kilometre and when I saw all the spectators, my friends and family on the beach in Margate, I had to put my goggles back on because I was starting to cry.

Reporter: And what are you planning on doing next?

Ross: I just want to stay warm and dry at the moment and I have to learn to use my feet again for walking. I basically just need to adapt to normal life again. I'm sure the next adventure will come along soon, though.

Reporter: It has been great talking to you, Ross. Thank you for coming in today.

Ross: Thank you too.

Adapted from: https://www.theguardian.com/uk-news/2018/nov/04/it-was-brutal-ross-edgley-completes-157-day-swim-around-britain

> You may now continue with the rest of the exam. Good luck!

Abschlussprüfung Englisch 2020

A Listening Comprehension

Part One

Listen to the news items and tick (✓) the right statements.
There is only one possible answer per statement.

News Item 1: Rapunzel   4 pts.

a) Natasha's hair is
   - ☐ longer than she is.
   - ☐ shorter than she is.
   - ☐ the same length as she is.

b) Natasha
   - ☐ washes her hair every day.
   - ☐ brushes her hair for one and a half hours every week.
   - ☐ has to hold her hair when walking.

c) Her family
   - ☐ call her Rapunzel.
   - ☐ love her hair.
   - ☐ suffer because of her hair.

d) Natasha can't go swimming because
   - ☐ her hair gets in the way.
   - ☐ the saltwater ruins her hair.
   - ☐ it takes hours to dry her hair.

News Item 2: Big Ben marathon runner   4 pts.

a) The fastest time for a runner dressed as a landmark is
   - ☐ 3 hours 54 minutes.
   - ☐ 3 hours 34 minutes.
   - ☐ 2 hours 59 minutes.

b) Marathon runner Lukas Bates could not finish the race because
   - ☐ of his costume.
   - ☐ of Big Ben.
   - ☐ of a volunteer.

c) In the end, Lukas
   - ☐ ran across the finishing line.
   - ☐ was helped by a race volunteer.
   - ☐ crawled over the line.

d) The world record for the fastest marathon time dressed as a landmark was set in
   - ☐ Berlin.
   - ☐ Lübeck.
   - ☐ London.

Part Two

Survey: Eating insects

Listen to these people talking about eating insects.
Who thinks what? Write the correct letters in the chart.
Be careful – there is one statement more than you need.

7 pts.

A Farming insects produces more protein than cattle.

B Farming insects is easier than traditional farming.

C Having insects in your diet is perfectly normal in other parts of the world.

D Don't say you'll never eat insects because you probably already are!

E There are certain health risks if you eat insects.

F Eating insects slows down climate change.

G Farming insects speeds up global warming faster than traditional farming.

H Insects are very nutritious!

Julie	David	Mia	Archie	Katy	Dora	Jenna

Part Three

Interview: Ross Edgley's Great British swim

Listen to the interview and write down the information needed.
Fill in only one detail per box.

10 pts.

how far Ross swam	
one of Ross' other world records	
when Ross started his swim	
one reason why the swim took longer	
swimming routine	
where Ross slept	
one difficulty Ross experienced	
what food he ate to get energy (one detail)	
how he felt when he arrived back in Margate	
current plans (one detail)	

B Reading Comprehension

1. Influence of social media on teens

❶ Dr Drew Pate is an expert on the emotional health of teenagers. Whenever he speaks to unhappy teens or their parents, one thing always comes up, he says. People are worried about sites like *Instagram, Facebook* or *Snapchat*. They wonder if such social media sites could be bad for teens. Parents ask if their children's constant use of social media is healthy. Doctors are hearing more and more about the damage done by social media, says Dr Pate. Most teens have probably been harmed by it in some way.

❷ Scientists are still trying to figure out how social media affect young people. So far, the evidence is mixed. Studies have shown that social media use can have a bad effect on some young people. Social media can also be helpful, however. They can help teens find support when they are struggling with life issues. They can provide them with a place to express themselves. Some teens are able to build real friendships with people they only know through social media.

❸ However, one recent study found major dangers. The more time teens spend on social media, the more likely they are to experience certain problems. Teens who use social media heavily are more likely to feel depressed. This is more serious than being sad. It is when you are unable to feel happy for a long period of time. Often, it is caused by imbalances of chemicals in the brain. In addition, social media could also affect your mood negatively.

❹ Scientists have also found a link between social media use and poor body image. People with a poor body image are convinced they are ugly or too fat. They worry about how they look all the time. Their condition can lead to eating disorders. A recent survey found that *Instagram* and *Snapchat* are the most likely to cause body-image problems. In particular, young women are at risk. They see endless photos of perfect bodies posted on those sites. Many of the photos are digitally edited to cover up people's imperfections. Teen girls can feel ugly when they measure themselves against these images.

❺ However, some experts point to studies that have found useful effects. One study found that social media help teenagers who play video games excessively. Heavy gamers who have a network of friends on social media seem to do better than those who play games a lot and don't have similar social networks. Those who have a network seem less likely to experience feelings of depression and worry, said researcher Michelle Colder Carras.

Studies send mixed messages on influence of social media on teens, Newsela vom 15.06.2017,
https://newsela.com/read/study-teenagers-emotional-health-social-media/id/31748/ (abgerufen am 21.10.2019, adaptiert)

Match the five correct headings to each part of the text (1–5).
Be careful – there are two headings more than you need.   5 pts.

A	CONTRADICTING DATA
B	BANNING PHOTOSHOP
C	PARENTAL CONTROL
D	COMPARISON TRAP
E	POSITIVE EFFECTS OF GAMING
F	PARENTAL WORRY
G	TENDENCY TO DEPRESSION

part of the text	❶	❷	❸	❹	❺
heading					

2. Why Scotland loves Haggis

Haggis is Scotland's most famous dish and was first made many hundred years ago. In those days it was essential for poorer people to use as much of an animal as possible. Some meat could be salted and dried for preservation. But if not eaten right away, internal organs quickly became unusable. Haggis made use of these organs by putting them into a useful natural bag – the animal's stomach – which could then be cooked immediately.

Traditionally, haggis takes the heart, liver and lungs of a sheep and mixes it with oatmeal, fat, spices, salt, pepper and meat juices. This mixture is then stuffed into a bag – today sometimes synthetic rather than a stomach, and no longer eaten as part of the dish – and cooked slowly for two to three hours at a low temperature. The result when placed on a plate looks a little like a balloon full of dark meat. It gives off a wonderful aroma when the bag is cut open to show the hot meat within.

In its early days, haggis served as a hearty meal for those on the move across Scotland: whisky-makers transporting liquid gold across majestic Highland hills, traders shipping their goods across the rough sea to the islands of Orkney and the Hebrides, shepherds driving their animals across the moors to feed hungry cities.

Though shepherds and whisky-makers no longer walk across modern-day Scotland, haggis is still eaten year-round – you can even buy it in tins or from fast food shops. But the one day all Scots turn to their beloved dish is Burns Night – a meal held every year on 25th January to celebrate the life and works of Scotland's national poet, Robert Burns, born in 1759.

20 The first Burns Night was celebrated in 1801, though held on 21st July when a group of his friends came together at Burns' childhood home in Ayrshire to celebrate his life and achievements on the fifth anniversary of the poet's death, rather than the birthday we celebrate today. These annual haggis suppers now range from informal parties of friends and family to large formal feasts.

25 A traditional menu will start with soup. This is followed by the haggis, which is the centrepiece of the evening. It is traditionally served with "neeps and tatties" – turnip[1] and potato – which can be simply boiled or mashed into a smooth puree that is perfect with the rough oaty texture of the haggis.

Along with the distinctive food, there will be whisky. Cooks can make a whisky-based sauce
30 to serve with the haggis, as well as serving the guests glasses of whisky to accompany the meal. It is up to the guests whether they want to sip the whisky or pour some of it over the haggis on their plate for a bit of extra traditional Scottish kick.

Burns Night celebrates other aspects of Scotland's history and culture, as well as its national dish. The feast traditionally begins with a bagpiper playing while the haggis is carried to the
35 table. There are also readings of classic texts such as a prayer in gratitude for the food.

The host closes the evening by inviting guests to stand and sing "Auld Lang Syne", based on a Burns poem and recognised by the Guinness Book of World Records as one of the most frequently sung songs in the English language.

Norman Miller: Why Scottish loves Haggis, BBC vom 24. 01. 2019, http://www.bbc.com/travel/story/20190123-why-scotland-loves-haggis (abgerufen am 24. 01. 2019, adaptiert).

1 turnip = a root vegetable

Tick (✓) the right statement. There is only one possible answer per statement.   10 pts.

a) In the past, especially poorer people needed to
- [ ] preserve their internal organs.
- [ ] salt and dry their haggis.
- [ ] eat their haggis at once.
- [ ] use almost all parts of an animal.

b) Haggis is cooked
- [ ] with whisky.
- [ ] in a balloon.
- [ ] gently.
- [ ] in a dish.

c) Originally, haggis was eaten
- [ ] by travellers.
- [ ] by Robert Burns.
- [ ] out of tins.
- [ ] in restaurants.

d) Today, you can buy this traditional dish
- [ ] only on Burns Night.
- [ ] only in tins.
- [ ] at any time.
- [ ] only in fast-food shops.

e) Robert Burns was a Scottish
- [ ] whisky-maker.
- [ ] trader.
- [ ] writer.
- [ ] cook.

f) Burns night was first celebrated
- [ ] five years after Burns had died.
- [ ] in 1759.
- [ ] on January 25th.
- [ ] on Robert Burns' birthday.

g) On Burns Night, haggis is normally served with
- [ ] soup.
- [ ] vegetables.
- [ ] meat.
- [ ] oats.

h) Cooks sometimes pour whisky
- [ ] into the soup.
- [ ] into the sauce.
- [ ] over the haggis.
- [ ] onto the plates.

i) Burns Night traditionally starts with
- [ ] Scottish music.
- [ ] Scottish history.
- [ ] a glass of whisky.
- [ ] a reading of the recipe.

k) "Auld Lang Syne" is usually sung
- [ ] at the beginning of the evening.
- [ ] at the end of the evening.
- [ ] when the haggis arrives.
- [ ] before reading a poem.

3. **Take your seats, everyone**

August "Auggie" Pullman is a 10-year-old boy who has just completed his first year at a new school. In the following extract, he and his friend Jack are attending the graduation ceremony.

Jack and I walked right behind a couple of sixth graders into the building, and then followed them to the auditorium.

Mrs. G was at the entrance, handing out the programs and telling kids where to go. […] The auditorium was huge inside. Big sparkly chandeliers. Red velvet walls. Rows and rows and rows of cushioned seats leading up to the giant stage. We walked down the wide aisle and followed the signs to the fifth-grade staging area, […] where Ms. Rubin was standing, waving us in as soon as we walked in the room. "Okay, kids, take your seats. Take your seats," she was saying, pointing to the rows of chairs. "Don't forget, you're sitting alphabetically. Come on, everybody, take your seats." Not too many kids had arrived yet, though, and the ones who had weren't listening to her. Me and Jack were sword-fighting with our rolled-up programs.

"Hey, guys." It was Summer walking over to us. She was wearing a light pink dress and, I think, a little makeup. "Wow, Summer, you look awesome," I told her, because she really did. "Really? Thanks, you do, too, Auggie." "Yeah, you look okay, Summer," said Jack, kind of matter-of-factly. And for the first time, I realized that Jack had a crush on her. "This is so exciting, isn't it?" said Summer. "Yeah, kind of," I answered, nodding.

"Oh man, look at this program," said Jack, scratching his forehead. "We're going to be here all freakin' day." […] "Why do you think that?" I asked.

"Because Mr. Jansen's speeches go on forever," said Jack. "He's even worse than Tushman!"

"My mom said she actually dozed off when he spoke last year," Summer added.

"What's the awards presentation?" I asked. "That's where they give medals to the biggest brainiacs," Jack answered. […] "Maybe *you'll* win this year," I joked. "Not unless they give awards for the most Cs[1]!" he laughed.

"Everybody, take your seats!" Ms. Rubin started yelling louder now, like she was getting annoyed that nobody was listening. "We have a lot to get through, so take your seats. Don't forget you're sitting in alphabetical order! A through G is the first row! […] Let's go, people."

"We should go sit down," said Summer, walking toward the front section. "You guys are definitely coming over my house after this, right?" I called out after her. "Definitely!" she said, taking her seat next to Ximena Chin. "When did Summer get so hot?" Jack muttered in my ear. "Shut up, dude[2]," I said, laughing as we headed toward the third row.

"Seriously, when did that happen?" he whispered, taking the seat next to mine. "Mr. Will!" Ms. Rubin shouted. "Last time I checked, *W* came between *R* and *Z*, yes?"

Jack looked at her blankly. "Dude, you're in the wrong row!" I said.

"I am?" And the face he made as he got up to leave, which was a mixture of looking completely confused and looking like he's just played a joke on someone, totally cracked me up.

Raquel J. Palacio: *Wonder*, Corgi books 2012, S. 294–297, adaptiert.

1 C = an average school mark
2 dude = US slang for a man or a boy

Answer the questions.

a) Describe the auditorium. (two details) — 2 pts.

b) In which grade are August, Jack and Summer? — 1 pt.

c) In what kind of order should the students sit? — 1 pt.

d) What does August say about Summer's appearance? — 1 pt.

e) Why do the kids think the ceremony will last a long time? — 1 pt.

f) Why does Ms. Rubin start shouting? — 1 pt.

g) How does Jack react when he is told he is in the wrong row? — 1 pt.

You cannot find the answers to the following questions directly in the text:

h) Why does Jack speak "kind of matter-of-factly" when he says that "Summer looks okay"? — 1 pt.

i) Which students is Jack referring to when he talks about the "biggest brainiacs"? — 1 pt.

C Use of Language

1. Mediation 12 pts.

The switched RV

Dein Onkel möchte seinen Urlaub im Dezember in Florida verbringen. Dazu hat er dort ein Wohnmobil (RV) für sich und seine Familie gebucht. Jetzt hat er eine E-Mail vom Vermieter erhalten. Da er nicht so gut Englisch spricht, leitet er dir die E-Mail weiter.

> To: ralf.klein@yuhuu.com
> From: JJKellyRVrental@Kelly.com
> Subject: Your RV Rental from 22nd to 31st December
> Sent: Friday, 13th October2019, 8:18 pm
>
> Dear Mr Klein,
> Thank you for choosing Cruise America and reserving an RV with us.
> You reserved the Standard RV for three people. We are very sorry, but this vehicle is no longer available. December is a very busy time for us and unfortunately we overbooked this RV.
> As a result we are willing to make the following offer: The Compact RV also sleeps three people comfortably with the table converting into a bed and the space over the driver's cabin extending into a double bed. Although this camper was not your first choice, we believe there are several reasons why this RV can be a better choice for you. If you are a first time renter, you will probably appreciate the narrower 2.3 meter width, which makes driving on narrow roads safer and easier and makes parking in any lot a breeze.
> We are also prepared to offer 300 free miles and a free kitchen kit, which would normally cost $110 and includes all the utensils that you need to cook and eat in your camper.
> We hope that you will consider our offer. If you have any questions, you can either call or send us an e-mail. Please let us know what you decide as soon as possible, as we have many requests for our vehicles for that time period.
> Best regards
> Joe Brown (Manager)

Dein Onkel bittet dich, ihm zu erklären, worum es in der E-Mail geht. Schreibe auf Deutsch die zwei Hauptanliegen auf, warum die Wohnmobilvermietung die E-Mail geschrieben hat:

_____ 1 pt.

_____ 1 pt.

Nenne ihm nun stichwortartig fünf weitere wichtige Informationen auf Deutsch:

❶ _____ 1 pt.

❷ _____ 1 pt.

❸ _____ 1 pt.

❹ _____ 1 pt.

❺ _____ 1 pt.

Nachdem du deinem Onkel die Informationen erklärt hast, schaut ihr euch im Internet die verschiedenen Wohnmobile an. Dein Onkel reagiert wie folgt:

> „Das Compact RV sieht ja viel kleiner aus – das ärgert mich dann doch ein bisschen. Wir müssen jetzt jeden Abend beide Betten umbauen und haben dann weniger Platz im Fahrzeug. Ich frage mich, wie viel Aufwand das jedes Mal bedeutet.
> Ich möchte jetzt auch gerne wissen, wie hoch der Innenraum ist und ob ich mit meinen 1,95 Metern aufrecht stehen kann. Das Badezimmer sieht auch kleiner aus. Ob ich da einigermaßen bequem duschen kann?
> Andererseits habe ich tatsächlich wenig Erfahrung mit Wohnmobilen und da ist das kleinere Fahrzeug vielleicht gar nicht so schlecht … Verbraucht der dann auch weniger Treibstoff?
> Auf jeden Fall ist mir klar, dass im Dezember Hochsaison ist und die Chancen, bei einem anderen Anbieter etwas zu finden, eher klein sind. Ich werde also auf jeden Fall das Angebot annehmen!"

Dein Onkel bittet dich, den Vermieter anzurufen und ihm seine Fragen und seine Entscheidung mitzuteilen. Du bereitest dich auf das Gespräch vor, indem du dir eine Liste auf Englisch anlegst.
Notiere dir zunächst auf Englisch das Hauptanliegen, warum dein Onkel dich bittet, dort anzurufen:

_____ 1 pt.

Notiere dann auf Englisch vier weitere wichtige Informationen, die du weitergeben sollst, oder Fragen, die du für deinen Onkel stellen wirst:

❶ _____ 1 pt.

❷ _____ 1 pt.

❸ _____ 1 pt.

❹ _____ 1 pt.

2. Words and structures

Read the text, then choose the correct words from the box to fill in the gaps. Use each word once only. There are more words than you need.   13 pts.

> about • are trained • at • crime • criminal • displays • how • in • minutes • participants' • quickly • residents • senses • sins • their • they're • training • used • who • whose

Police museum[1]

Police shows on TV are filled with high-speed car chases and crimes solved quickly – within a few (1) _____. But that is not a typical day for a real-life police officer. At the new National Law Enforcement Museum in Washington, interactive (2) _____ invite visitors to use their (3) _____ of sight, hearing, touch and smell.

In that way, they can learn about the way police officers, detectives and forensic scientists do (4) _____ work.

Visitors can discover how footprints and DNA help solve crimes. They can also sit in a real police car that officers (5) _____ on the streets. There, the visitors can learn (6) _____ the meaning of different emergency light patterns and sirens.

Visitors will (7) _____ learn that crime-solving is a team effort, not only within one police department, but among many law enforcement agencies across the country. For example, six agencies worked together on a national park graffiti case. There is also a video of how dogs (8) _____ before they join the so-called K-9 units, where dogs are partners of police officers. Visitors learn which dogs are good for tracking the bad guys and which dogs are better (9) _____ sniffing out drugs.

Visitors (10) _____ are at least twelve years old can try the same training scenarios and equipment used in professional law enforcement classes. Short videos test the (11) _____ abilities to observe accurately and think quickly before reacting. The exercises give an understanding of what officers face on a daily basis. Because every community is different, the museum shows (12) _____ the needs and challenges of different communities are being addressed. There are programs to minimize problems and reduce (13) _crime_____, while increasing trust between residents and police.

<small>Ann Cameron Siegal: New museum lets visitors walk in the shoes of a police officer, *Washington Post* vom 28. 11. 2018, https://www.washingtonpost.com/lifestyle/kidspost/a-look-into-the-new-national-law-enforcement-museum/2018/11/27/f4928072-f1ae-11e8-aeea-b85fd44449f5_story.html (adaptiert),
From The Washington Post. © 2018 The Washington Post. All rights reserved. Used under license.</small>

---

1 Der Originaltext des Artikels aus der *Washington Post* lautet:

Police shows on TV are filled with high-speed car chases and crimes solved in a matter of minutes. But that's not a typical day for a real-life police officer. To get a more accurate picture, head to the new National Law Enforcement Museum in Washington. Interactive exhibits there invite visitors to use their senses of sight, hearing, touch and smell in gathering information the way police, detectives and forensic scientists do.

Explore how footprints and DNA, or genetic material, help solve crimes. Sit in an actual police cruiser as you learn the meaning of different emergency light patterns and sirens.

"It's a walk-in-their-shoes experience," said Julie Bell, the museum's manager of school programs.

Let's look at a few exhibits.

The Web of Law Enforcement: You'll quickly learn that crime-solving is a team effort, not only within one department, but among agencies across the country. The FBI, Secret Service, Coast Guard and Postal […] Inspection Service are just some of the law enforcement groups helping local police when needed. For example, six agencies worked together on a national park graffiti case.

K-9 units: See a video of how dogs are trained to join K-9 units. Test your ability to smell and identify various scents. Learn which breeds are better at tracking the bad guys while others are better at sniffing out drugs. Why are Chihuahuas better at some tasks than German shepherds?

The Training Simulator: Those age 12 and older can try the same training scenarios and equipment used in professional law enforcement classes in which police try to resolve difficult situations. Short videos, based on real police encounters, test participants' abilities to observe accurately and think quickly before reacting.

The exercises give an understanding of what officers face on a daily basis.

"Many kids first think it's like a video game," said Alan Davis, an educator and retired New York police officer. "They soon realize that real-life split-second decision-making isn't easy, and they freeze. For real police, there are no second chances." […]

Five Communities (current programs): Every community is different. Learn how the needs and challenges of five communities are being addressed. These communities' goals are to develop programs to minimize problems and reduce crime, while increasing trust between residents and police. What might work in your neighborhood? There's a place for visitors to share their thoughts.

As Luther Reynolds, police chief in Charleston, South Carolina, told the museum, "There is no department in this country that doesn't have the room to get better."

D Text Production

Choose one of the following tasks and write about 150 words.
Count your words and write the number at the end of the text.

25 pts.

What is the story behind the picture?

Imagine you see the boys sitting near you.

Write a text and include at least four of the following aspects:
- Who are they?
- Where are they?
- What are the boys doing?
- What will happen next?
- What are the boys' thoughts?

or

The importance of travelling

On the Internet you come across an English writing competition. The topic is "The importance of travelling". You decide to enter this competition.

Write a text and include at least four of the following aspects:
- Which countries or places have you visited/would you like to visit?
- What is important when travelling?
- Why is travelling good for you?
- What was the most exciting thing that happened to you?
- Are there any negative aspects of travelling?

Hessen Realschule – Englisch
Jahrgang 2021

Listening Comprehension – Transcripts

Hello, this is the listening exam. I am going to give you the instructions for the test. There are three parts to the listening exam. At the beginning of each part, you'll hear this sound: ◀
You may write down your answers at any point during the listening exam.

Part One

In part one you will hear two news items. You will hear the news items twice. Before listening to each news item, you will have 20 seconds to read the tasks. You now have 20 seconds to read the tasks for news item one. *(20 seconds break)* You are now going to hear the first news item for the first time. After a short break, you will hear the news item again. ◀

News Item 1: Pancake race

No one is quite certain how the pancake race in Olney, Buckinghamshire, started, but six hundred years later, the tradition is still going strong. The race, which takes place on the day before the beginning of Lent, began in 1445 after a stressed housewife had to run to church because she was late for the service.
After a break during the Second World War, the race was revived again in 1948 by the vicar of Olney. When he was cleaning out a cupboard, he came across some old photos, which had been taken in the 1920s and 30s, of women running with frying pans. He decided to hold the race once again and called for volunteers. In response, 13 runners appeared that year and the people of Olney enjoyed this traditional and colourful festivity once again.
The rules are simple. Only women who are over 18 and have lived in Olney for over three months can enter. Participants must wear a skirt, a headscarf and carry a frying pan. The race is about 400 yards, or about 365 metres, from the marketplace to the church door. Amy Butler won the race last year in seventy seconds.

Adapted from: Pancake Day: 'World's oldest' race still going in Olney, 5 March 2019, SectionBBC, NewsSubsectionBeds, Herts & Bucks, https://www.bbc.co.uk/news/av/uk-england-beds-bucks-herts-47456655

You now have 20 seconds to read the tasks for news item two. *(20 seconds break)* You are now going to hear the second news item for the first time. After a short break, you will hear news item two again. ◀

News Item 2: Missing black cat

A black cat which went missing six years ago has been reunited with his shocked owners in time for Halloween. Clyde escaped and disappeared days after his owners moved to a new home in Bradford-on-Avon in Wiltshire in 2013. But on Wednesday, the homeless, micro-chipped cat was brought into the veterinary centre in the town and identified as Clyde.
Owner Mel Sargeant, who still lives locally, said that he was still in total shock. He and his wife, however, were overjoyed to get their black cat back on Halloween. Mrs Sargeant said they had got Clyde and his sister Bonnie from a rescue centre 15 years ago. When he went missing, the couple searched the streets. They looked everywhere, put photos up, but there was nothing until 24 hours ago, when the vet phoned up to say that a cat had been handed in. They rushed down to the vet's and got the surprise of their lives.
Mr Harris, the vet, said the cat had been brought into them after having been seen hanging around outside an old people's home. It is thought Clyde had been there for the last four years. He was fed by staff and people called him George. Mrs Sargeant recognised him straight away by his bright eyes.
However, Clyde and Bonnie haven't met each other yet and Mrs Sargeant hopes that Bonnie will be happy to meet her long-lost brother again.

Missing black cat has Halloween reunion with owner after six years, BBC 31 October 2019, https://www.bbc.co.uk/news/uk-england-wiltshire-50245849

Part Two

> In part two a reporter is carrying out a survey. You will hear this twice. Before listening, you will have 40 seconds to read the task. You now have 40 seconds to read the task. *(40 seconds break)*
> You are now going to hear the survey for the first time. After a short break, you will hear the survey again. ◀

Survey: Video gaming

Reporter: Today's topic is video gaming. Video games are not only popular among kids, adults also play video games regularly. This morning, I spoke to students and teachers from Huntington School in York. I asked them what they thought of video gaming. Here is a selection of their answers.

Kieran: Hi, my name is Kieran. I just love video games! At the moment, I'm playing *Legend of Zelda*. It's just great! For me, video games allow me to relax. I can forget about school stress or any other problems I might have and just slip into a fantasy world where I can be someone else. That's so cool!

Helena: Good morning. It's Helena here. I also have a games console, I've got an XBox One. I like the sort of games where you must make decisions and solve problems. You have to act fast and multitask. I think this helps me in daily life too. I can analyse problems faster and make decisions more quickly.

Nina: Hello, I'm Nina. There may be some positive effects of gaming, but when I think of the gamers in my class, they are the ones whose grades suffer. They spend all their free time on their PS4, or whatever it's called, playing through the night sometimes, and then they forget their homework or are half-dead in the lessons.

Jordan: My name is Jordan. Hi. I like the game *Battlefield*. Yeah, it might be a bit violent, but it's also a really fascinating game based on real historic events. I've learned loads about World War 2 and how terrible it was. It really has improved my knowledge of history.

Mrs Townsend: My name is Mrs Townsend and I am sure it's not just kids who are at risk because of computer games. I'm thinking of my brother-in-law, who has a regular job, a wife and three children. Every evening he's online playing *World of Warcraft*. He plays for hours and hours. If you ask me, he's losing touch with his children. They hardly talk to each other anymore and when they do, they always argue. His relationship to my sister has got worse too. It worries me.

Annie: Hi, my name is Annie and I think some video games can improve your social skills. Take the game *Destiny 2*, for example. To be successful at this game, you have to build online social networks to help you complete goals together. I think that this is the same skill that young people need to build career networks so that their careers can advance well.

Macaulay: My name is Macaulay and video games are incredibly realistic nowadays and a lot of them are really violent. There are studies that show that first person shooter games can increase aggressive behaviour. This isn't true for everyone, but some people find it hard to act normally after playing violent video games.

Reporter: Thank you for your contributions. Keep calling with your opinions, we'll have an update later.

Part Three

> In part three you will hear an interview. You will hear the interview twice. Before listening to the interview, you will have 30 seconds to read the task. You now have 30 seconds to read the task.
>
> *(30 seconds break)* You are now going to hear the interview for the first time. After a short break, you will hear the interview again. ◀

Interview: Night rider

Reporter: Our guest in the studio today is Sunny, a fifty-five-year-old Nigerian who has spent almost 21 years riding London buses at night. Good morning, Sunny.

Sunny: Good morning.

Reporter: Sunny, tell us, please: Why have you spent so much time aboard London buses?

Sunny: I came to Britain in 1998. In my home country Nigeria, I was a political prisoner because I had campaigned for democracy. I had been given the death sentence, but my family and my friends helped me to escape to the UK. However, when I arrived in London, I wasn't allowed to stay.

Reporter: What did you do?

Sunny: I couldn't go back to Nigeria, so I became an illegal immigrant. And that is why I was homeless for over twenty years.

Reporter: But why did you spend the nights on buses? Why didn't you go to a centre for homeless people?

Sunny: I discovered that the London night buses were safer and warmer than the streets and the centres were often overcrowded.

Reporter: So you took to the buses. Tell us how you did it, Sunny.

Sunny: At no later than 9 pm, I would get on the first of three or four buses and travel through the night. I soon discovered which buses were the best for a good rest.

Reporter: You make it sound so easy but sleeping on different buses at night – every night – must be very challenging.

Sunny: It is, but I soon worked out that the best place to sleep was downstairs at the back of the bus. Most families stay downstairs on a double-decker bus and there is less trouble near the bus driver. It is still not easy to sleep, though – the constant movement of the bus, the neon lights, the noisy travellers and the humming sound of the engine all make sleeping quite difficult.

Reporter: And you did this for twenty years. Now you are allowed to stay in Britain. What changed?

Sunny: Well, as a rule, after living in the UK continuously for twenty years, you have the right to stay. The problem was that I didn't have any proof that I had lived in the UK for over twenty years. There was no record of me living anywhere.

Reporter: What did you do?

Sunny: I asked one of the friendliest bus drivers to write a letter of support for me and the church where I had volunteered over the years also helped me. They found some old photos which showed me at some charity events.

Reporter: Ah, so then you could prove that you had been in the UK for twenty years.

Sunny: That's correct, and I now have the right to a home and I am allowed to work in the UK. I live in a flat in the south of London. I have been very lucky.

Reporter: Sunny, thank you for sharing your story with us today.

Adapted from: Venetia Menzies: Night rider: 21 years sleeping on a London bus, BBC 12 January 2020, https://www.bbc.co.uk/news/stories-50459821

> You may now continue with the rest of the exam. Good luck!

Abschlussprüfung Englisch 2021

A Listening Comprehension

Part One

Listen to the news items and tick (✓) the right statements.
There is only one possible answer per statement.

News Item 1: Pancake race   4 pts.

a) The pancake race takes place ____ Lent.
- [ ] before
- [ ] during
- [ ] after

b) In 1948, the race was held again after the vicar
- [ ] had cleaned all the cupboards.
- [ ] had discovered some old photographs.
- [ ] came running with a frying pan.

c) To take part in the race, you must
- [ ] carry a skirt.
- [ ] be male and over 18.
- [ ] wear something on your head.

d) The race
- [ ] finishes at the church.
- [ ] is about 400 metres long.
- [ ] is about 365 yards long.

News Item 2: Missing black cat   4 pts.

a) Clyde went missing after his owners had moved
- [ ] away from Braford-on-Avon.
- [ ] at Halloween.
- [ ] to a new house.

b) Clyde originally came from a rescue centre
- [ ] 6 years ago.
- [ ] 15 years ago.
- [ ] in 2013.

c) The black cat had been
- [ ] found inside an old people's home.
- [ ] fed by someone called George.
- [ ] looked after at an old people's home.

d) The owner Mrs Sargeant said she saw it was Clyde because
- [ ] he has shiny eyes.
- [ ] he looks like his sister.
- [ ] he has a microchip.

Part Two

Survey: Video gaming

Listen to these people talking about video gaming.
Who thinks what? Write the correct letters in the chart.
Be careful – there is one statement more than you need.

7 pts.

A Video games can affect your school performance.

B Gamers are sometimes isolated from their families.

C Playing video games lets me forget my problems in the real world.

D I've learned a lot of interesting historical facts through video games.

E Video games have a bad effect on your career.

F You need the same sort of people skills for some online games that you need at work.

G Computer games improve decision-making speed.

H I think some people are definitely angrier after playing a "shoot-em-up" game.

Kieran	Helena	Nina	Jordan	Mrs Townsend	Annie	Macaulay

Part Three

Interview: Night rider

Listen to the interview and write down the information about Sunny.
Fill in only one detail per box.

10 pts.

Sunny's age	
year he came to Britain	
why he had to leave Nigeria	
why he spent the night on buses	
best place to sleep on a double-decker bus	
why it was difficult to sleep on a bus (two details)	
why Sunny did not have the right to stay in the UK	
what a bus driver did to help	
how he feels today	

B Reading Comprehension

1. Banksy

❶ Banksy is an anonymous English street and graffiti artist as well as a political artist. His provocative work was first discovered around the south of England, including in London, Brighton and Bristol. Banksy's works are known for their criticism of society and its conditions. Banksy is well-known for painting large graffiti murals in cities without any official permission.

❷ It is widely accepted that Banksy's street career began in the early 1990s in Bristol. Like many street artists, he adopted common repeated motifs such as apes, policemen, soldiers, children or elderly people to show his special influence in public spaces. However, his favourite subjects are rats. In his work, these nocturnal creatures can be understood as a sort of self-portrait because he also completes his masterpieces under the cover of darkness.

❸ In August 2004, Banksy produced tons of fake British £10 notes, worth £1,000,000. On the notes, he replaced the picture of the Queen's head with that of Diana, Princess of Wales, and changed the text "Bank of England" into "Banksy of England". Then someone threw several of these notes into a crowd at the Notting Hill Carnival. Some people even tried to spend the fake money in local shops. He then felt compelled to stop the distribution. The individual notes have since been selling on the Internet for about £200 each.

❹ Throughout the 2000s, Banksy held many exhibitions in the UK and US and became prominent after celebrities had begun to buy his pieces. Suddenly, Banksy's works were fetching tens of thousands of pounds at auction houses and the mysterious street artist was world-famous. Creating an air of mystery around himself helped him to become one of the most successful artists of his generation. When an American magazine estimated Banksy's wealth at around £14 million ($26 million), he showed regret, saying he wished his works were worthless.

❺ Banksy continues to keep his true identity a secret and the reason for this might be that he wants to avoid prosecution for creating illegal graffiti. Little is known of his youth. He is believed to have been born in Bristol, in around 1974. Scientists at Queen Mary University of London claim to have found out who Banksy is by using geographic profiling. This technique is normally used for catching serial criminals. Like others before, they believe a former student of the Bristol Cathedral School, Robin Gunningham, is the artist. But the man himself denies it. There has also been speculation that rather than being a single person, Banksy is a team of seven artists.

https://www.theartstory.org/artist/banksy/life-and-legacy/
https://www.thesun.co.uk/news/3309415/who-banksy-how-make-money/
https://www.telegraph.co.uk/art/what-to-see/who-is-banksy-and-what-is-his-real-name-the-man-behind-the-myths/
https://www.thesun.co.uk/news/7437564/banksy-reveals-how-he-installed-self-destruct-device-into-girl-with-balloon-artwork-years-before-1m-artwork-was-shredded-at-auction/.
https://www.biography.com/artist/banksy

https://web.archive.org/web/20090215230943/
http://briansewell.com/artist/b-artist/banksy/banksy-biography.html
https://www.news.com.au/lifestyle/real-life/who-is-banksy-worldfamous-but-mysterious-street-artist-reignites-search-for-his-true-identity/news-story/38a3a03793de86e473f2cbc757ab652f

Match the five correct headings to each part of the text (1–5).
Be careful – there are two headings more than you need.   5 pts.

A	SUCCESS DESPITE ANONYMITY
B	CREATING LEGAL GRAFFITI
C	IDENTITY REMAINS UNCLEAR
D	REGRETTING HIS WORKS
E	POLITICAL MESSAGES
F	ANIMALS AS SYMBOLS
G	COOL FORGERIES

part of the text	❶	❷	❸	❹	❺
heading					

2. Young people and working attitudes

1. The number of teenagers working in Saturday jobs has almost halved in the past 20 years. Activities such as sitting at cash desks, stacking shelves and delivering newspapers have gone out of fashion and more and more people are now going online to earn cash.

Only one in four 16- and 17-year-olds takes up paid traditional work, compared with 48 % in 1999. According to the thinktank *Resolution Foundation,* the number of adults – now 3.4 million – who have never had a paid job is also increasing.

Some young people go online to make money, with 2 million young adults signed up to the fashion trading site *Depop*. It claims its most successful sellers earn £2,000 a month – far more than the £250 a typical teenager would earn monthly working Saturdays.

10. Researchers also believe many young people are delaying the start of traditional work because they face longer working lives and want to focus more strongly on studies. But employers warn that the decrease in teenage part-time work is leaving many of them unprepared for the realities of working life.

"This lack of work experience can create longer-term problems, particularly if they hit other life milestones, such as getting married or having a baby, or ill-health before their careers have started," said Laura Gardiner, the *Resolution Foundation*'s research director.

Many of the UK's most successful people have spoken publicly about their Saturday jobs: the London mayor Sadiq Khan worked on a building site, the business woman Karren Brady worked in a hair salon and the journalist Robert Peston cleaned freezers in a frozen food shop. The jobs that 16- and 17-year-olds are most likely to do include waiting tables, helping in restaurant and hotel kitchens and working as shop assistants.

"School leavers and university graduates coming into the workplace often lack the key skills they need. They are not tough enough, have no team spirit and do not know how to behave in a working environment," said Amy Leonard, the chief executive of the *Transformation Trust,* which helps disadvantaged teenagers get into work. "It's not just about developing the right skills. It's also about explaining the world of work and helping young adults to develop the confidence to take that next step from education into work."

According to a recent survey, almost half of the employers believe that young people leaving school, college or university are not ready for work.

Last year, another study found out that 11 % of young people bought and sold clothes and products online because they found this line of work more flexible and also because there were simply no traditional jobs in their area.

The general rise in the number of people who have never worked means that a third of people who are currently out of work have never been employed, compared to a fifth in the late 1990s.

This trend is not the result of people deciding to live on welfare benefits, the *Resolution Foundation* said, but due to the fact that university and college students worked less, had a longer break between leaving full-time education and getting paid work and the decline of the teenage Saturday job.

Robert Booth: Proportion of young people in Saturday jobs halves in 20 years, *The Guardian* vom 04. 01. 2020, https://www.theguardian.com/society/2020/jan/04/proportion-of-young-people-in-saturday-jobs-halves-in-20-years, © Guardian News & Media Ltd 2021

Tick (✓) the right statement. There is only one possible answer per statement. 10 pts.

a) The number of teenagers working on Saturdays has ____ in the last 20 years.
- [ ] grown
- [ ] doubled
- [ ] increased
- [ ] decreased

b) One in four 16- and 17-year-olds
- [ ] works online.
- [ ] has never worked.
- [ ] has a traditional job.
- [ ] stacks shelves.

c) A typical Saturday job will bring in about _____ a month.
- [ ] £20
- [ ] £48
- [ ] £250
- [ ] £2,000

d) Many teenagers do not want to start working too soon because they
- [ ] want to postpone their studies.
- [ ] want to concentrate on their education.
- [ ] will not be prepared for working life.
- [ ] will not work for long enough.

e) Not having a Saturday job can create problems because teenagers
- [ ] have no work experience.
- [ ] have no money.
- [ ] are not prepared for online work.
- [ ] struggle with long-term milestones.

f) As a teenager, the London mayor worked
- [ ] in a food shop.
- [ ] in a restaurant.
- [ ] at a construction site.
- [ ] at a hairdresser's.

g) According to Amy Leonard, young people starting work
- [ ] know how to behave in a working environment.
- [ ] can work in a team at the workplace.
- [ ] can explain the world of work.
- [ ] need help to adjust to the workplace.

h) Many _____ think school leavers are not prepared properly for work.
- [ ] executives
- [ ] employers
- [ ] researchers
- [ ] entrepreneurs

i) Online work allows young people to
- [ ] be more flexible.
- [ ] try a traditional job.
- [ ] work locally.
- [ ] develop key skills.

k) A third of all unemployed people
- [ ] are socially disadvantaged.
- [ ] have always worked.
- [ ] have bought and sold clothes online.
- [ ] have never had a job.

3. Molly's first day at work

So, this is probably my own fault [...], but I'm actually a little nervous about starting work. Even though this isn't a brain surgery residency. I'm very glad this isn't a brain surgery residency. I don't think anyone wants me operating on their brain right now, or ever.

Especially because my hands are shaking – just a little – on the door handle.

The store looks the same as it always does – which is to say, it looks like Zooey Deschanel[1] exploded into five thousand tablecloths and painted plates and letterpress notecards. It's called Bissel. [...] Like the Yiddish word, meaning "a little bit". As in, good luck only spending a bissel of money when you walk into Bissel. Good luck not spending your entire paycheck on a bissel of handcrafted artisan jewelry.

I can't believe I'm walking into Bissel as an employee. I'm an *employee*.

Deborah and Ari Wertheim, the owners, are behind the counter, and I feel this wave of shyness. "Hi," I say, and my voice comes out comically high. Squeaky Molly. Super professional. Deborah looks up from the register[2]. "Molly – hi! Oh great, you're here." She presses both palms against the counter, beaming. "We are so, so glad you're joining us." She's intensely nice. They both are. That's the main thing I remember about the Wertheims from my interview. They're nice in the way therapists are – like, you get the impression they'd be up for hearing your thoughts about life and humanity. They're married, and they're a perfect matched set: tall and big-boned, with thick-framed glasses. Ari's bald, and Deborah has this kind of wild black hair she wears knotted into a messy bun. Or sometimes two meatball Sailor Moon buns, even though she's probably in her forties. I really love that. Also, they both have these brightly colored, amazingly intricate tattoos all up and down their arms. Literally, they are the two coolest adult humans on the planet, or at least in Maryland. "Hmm, so I guess we probably went over most of this stuff at the interview. You remember how to use the register?" I nod, even though I definitely don't remember how to use the register.

"Cool. Though the register is being an asshole today, so I'll probably stick you in the back room with Reid. And he can kind of show you around. You've met Reid?" "I don't think so." "Oh, I'll introduce you." [...] Deborah comes back a minute later with a guy I've actually seen here before. He's tall and kind of big, in that way people describe as *husky*. His shirt has a map of Middle Earth on it. And his sneakers are so electric white, they're either brand-new, or he puts them in the laundry.

"Molly, this is Reid. Reid, Molly." "Hi," he says, smiling shyly. "Hi." I smile back.

Deborah turns to me. "Molly, you're going to be a senior, right?" I nod.

"Perfect! You guys are the same age. I bet you have a lot in common."

Classic adult logic. Reid and I are vaguely the same age, so of course we're basically soul mates. [...] "You've been working here for years, right?" I say. "I've seen you before." [...] "Yeah, I'm here all the time. Kind of unavoidable." He shrugs. "My parents."

"Your parents?" "Ari and Deborah."

I clap a hand over my mouth. "Ari and Deborah are your parents?" "You didn't know that?" He looks amused. I shake my head slowly. "Okay. You just blew my mind."

"Really?" He laughs. "Why?"

"Because! I don't know. Deborah and Ari just seem so ..." Punkrock and badass and not into Lord of the Rings. "They have tattoos," I say finally.

He nods. "They do."

I just gape for a minute. He laughs again. "You seem so surprised." [...]

Becky Albertalli: *The Upside of Unrequited*, New York, 1. Auflage 2017, S. 24–28, adaptiert

1 Zooey Deschanel = an American actress and singer known for her creative outfits
2 register = the machine in a shop that holds the money

Answer the questions.

a) What happens to Molly when she is nervous?   1 pt.

b) What can you buy in the store Bissel?   1 pt.

c) What happens to Molly when she feels shy?   1 pt.

d) Name two details that illustrate that the Wertheims are a "perfect matched set".   2 pts.

e) Why does Deborah think that Molly and Reid have a lot in common?   1 pt.

f) Why is Molly surprised to discover that Ari and Deborah are Reid's parents? (Name two details.)   2 pts.

You cannot find the answers to the following questions directly in the text:

g) Molly says that the Wertheims are "nice in the way therapists are". What does she mean by that?   1 pt.

_____

h) Why does Molly claim to be able to use the register even though she can't?   1 pt.

_____

C Use of Language

1. **Mediation**   15 pts.

   Interview with a YouTuber

   Sabine, eine Mitschülerin aus deinem Jahrgang, soll für die Schülerzeitung eine YouTuberin aus den USA interviewen. Da sie nicht so gut Englisch spricht und sich nicht recht traut, bittet sie dich, sie zu begleiten.
   Vermittle zwischen Sabine und der YouTuberin. Ergänze den folgenden Dialog mit den wichtigsten Informationen in der jeweils geforderten Sprache.

   Sabine: Nochmals danke, dass du mir hilfst! Ich bin ganz aufgeregt. OK, frag doch bitte als Erstes, wie lange sie schon Videos macht und warum sie damit überhaupt angefangen hat.

   Du [Englisch]: _____ 2 pts.

   _____

   YouTuberin: Ah, for quite a while now. I started my YouTube channel about four years ago. And I didn't think of money or fame, as people sometimes think. I did it because I've always loved to entertain. I guess it is just the right thing for me to do.

   Du [Deutsch]: _____ 3 pts.

   _____

   _____

   Sabine: Ah, so lange schon! Das hätte ich jetzt nicht erwartet. Kann sie denn davon leben?

   Du [Englisch]: _____ 1 pt.

   _____

   YouTuberin: Haha, I can only dream of that. I do it in addition to my regular job.

   Du [Deutsch]: _____ 1 pt.

   _____

Sabine: Oh, das wundert mich, dass sie das zeitlich hinbekommt. Ich habe gelesen, dass die Produktion von Videos sehr zeitaufwendig ist. Was motiviert sie denn dann, immer neue Inhalte zu produzieren?

Du [Englisch]: _____ 1 pt.

_____

YouTuberin: What drives me? That's really easy to explain! I do it because it is great fun. For example, I really enjoy the process of coming up with ideas, filming, and editing. Seeing the responses from my viewers is what really keeps me going.

Du [Deutsch]: _____ 3 pts.

_____

_____

Sabine: Toll! Das klingt sehr überzeugend! Ich kann ihre Begeisterung spüren. Frage sie doch mal nach typischen Reaktionen ihrer Fans. Ich finde das sehr interessant.

Du [Englisch]: _____ 1 pt.

_____

YouTuberin: I love communicating with my viewers. Some people have sent me pictures of drawings they've made for me. Many send me fanmail telling me how much my videos have inspired them to try something new. It's times like those that make my efforts worthwhile.

Du [Deutsch]: _____ 2 pts.

_____

_____

Sabine: Faszinierend. Das zeigt, wie wichtig ihre Videos für sie sind. Das war ein sehr informatives Gespräch. Danke ihr bitte dafür und sage ihr, dass sie heute einen neuen Fan gewonnen hat.

Du [Englisch]: _____ 1 pt.

_____

YouTuberin: No problem, that was fun! Great to hear – see you on YouTube then. Bye and take care.

2. Words and structures

Read the text, then tick (✓) the correct words. 10 pts.

How Garfield telephones ended up on French beaches

A thirty-year-old environmental mystery has finally been solved. __1__ the 1980s, pieces of plastic telephones that look like Garfield – the lazy cartoon cat – have been washing up on beaches in France.

__2__ living in Brittany, in the northwest of France, have picked up hundreds of pieces of the bright orange phones from beaches along the Atlantic coast. But for three decades, no one knew where the phones __3__ from.

__4__ March 22nd, a group of volunteers from *Ar Viltansoù,* a coastal clean-up organization, along with two journalists from *#AlertePollution,* finally detected the source of the phones. They discovered a broken shipping container and parts of several Garfield phones inside a rocky sea cave. The cave is hard to find and can only be reached when the sea is low.

Supinda Duke-Aiton / Alamy Stock Foto

Shipping containers are used to move things __5__ food, clothing and other items across the sea. Cargo ships carry hundreds of the huge steel containers from the countries where the goods are made or grown to the countries where they will be sold.

__6__ knows for sure how the shipping container full of Garfield phones ended up in the cave. People who live in the area say that the phones first showed up on beaches after a big storm in the early 1980s. The container probably fell __7__ a ship during the storm, but nobody ever reported that it was missing.

The Garfield phones have become a symbol of the problem of ocean __8__.

Fabien Boileau is the director of *Iroise Marine Natural Park,* __9__ the cave with the phones is located. He said the Garfield phones help people to understand that plastic trash __10__ break down in the ocean. Some of the colourful plastic pieces still look almost new, even though they washed overboard more than 30 years ago.

Monique Conrod: How Garfield Phones Ended Up On French Beaches, Teaching Kids News vom 14.04. 2019, https://teachingkidsnews.com/2019/04/14/how-garfield-phones-ended-up-on-french-beaches/

1. ☐ When ☐ For ☐ Since ☐ Because	2. ☐ People ☐ Peoples ☐ People's ☐ Peoples'	3. ☐ was coming ☐ were coming ☐ are coming ☐ will be coming	4. ☐ Of ☐ At ☐ In ☐ On
5. ☐ as ☐ unlike ☐ like ☐ similar	6. ☐ They ☐ Anybody ☐ Everybody ☐ Nobody	7. ☐ out ☐ of ☐ off ☐ over	8. ☐ polluted ☐ pollutant ☐ pollution ☐ polluting

9.	☐ where	10.	☐ doesn't
	☐ were		☐ don't
	☐ while		☐ hadn't
	☐ who		☐ haven't

D Text Production

Choose one of the following tasks and write about 150 words.
Count your words and write the number at the end of the text.   25 pts.

What is the story behind the picture?

Imagine you see this couple.

Write a text and include at least four of the following aspects:
- Who are they?
- Where are they?
- What happened before?
- How do they feel?
- What will happen next?

auremar / AdobeStock

or

Digital detox

You make a bet with your best friend:
Live without the Internet and your telephone for two weeks.

Write a text and include at least four of the following aspects:
- What do you miss most?
- How do you feel?
- How do you spend your days?
- Will you change something after the two weeks?
- What must you do if you lose the bet?

**Hessen Realschule – Englisch
Jahrgang 2022**

Listening Comprehension – Transcripts

Hello, this is the listening exam. I am going to give you the instructions for the test. There are three parts to the listening exam. At the beginning of each part, you'll hear this sound: ◀
You may write down your answers at any point during the listening exam.

Part One

In part one you will hear two news items. You will hear the news items twice. Before listening to each news item, you will have 20 seconds to read the tasks. You now have 20 seconds to read the tasks for news item one. *(20 seconds break)* You are now going to hear the first news item for the first time. After a short break, you will hear the news item again. ◀

News Item 1: Famous auctions

Many people would like to have a Hollywood souvenir in their homes and what better way to do that than by owning a piece of equipment used in a movie? The craze started in the 1970s, when the president of MGM Studios decided to auction off thousands of items from past films in order to save some money. Here is a selection of the most popular objects.

In 2014, Aragorn's sword from *The Lord of the Rings* was put up for auction. It sold for an amazing $510,000, almost double the estimated price. Clothes and shoes worn in famous films also do well at auctions. Dorothy's shoes from *The Wizard of Oz* sold for an incredible $660,000 in the year 2000. In the book, which came first, the shoes were actually silver but the colour was changed to ruby red for the film so they would stand out better against the yellow brick road. In 2020, a gun used by James Bond actor Sean Connery sold for a record $256,000 in Los Angeles. The semi-automatic pistol, a Walther PP, was used by Sean Connery in his first Bond film *Dr. No* in 1962. The buyer wishes to remain anonymous, but he has been described as an American who has seen every Bond movie with his children.

Adapted from: https://www.catawiki.com/stories/4415-top-10-most-memorable-movie-props-at-auction (last accessed on 18.02.2021). https://variety.com/2020/artisans/news/sean-connery-james-bond-dr-no-pistol-auction-1234845489/ (last accessed on 09.09.2021).

You now have 20 seconds to read the tasks for news item two. *(20 seconds break)* You are now going to hear the second news item for the first time. After a short break, you will hear news item two again. ◀

News Item 2: Cicadas

You recognize that sound, don't you? Yes, it's the buzzing of cicadas. Fifteen US states are about to be invaded by billions or even trillions of these insects, including New York, Illinois, Georgia and New Jersey. The noisy, red-eyed members of Brood X, which have been underground for the past 17 years, will come out as soon as the conditions are right. The ground temperatures must be 64 degrees Fahrenheit, or 17 degrees Celsius, and it must be a humid night, but free of rain and wind. Though they don't bite or sting, the clouds of insects are pretty impressive. Male cicadas together can sing at a 105 decibels, which is louder than a lawn-mower. They sing to attract a partner and once they have mated, the female cicadas will then lay their eggs in the branches of young trees. The next generation of young cicadas drop down to the ground at the end of the summer and burrow into the soil, where they will spend the next 17 years feeding on plant roots. Once their work is completed, their parents die and become a tasty treat for cats, dogs, birds, and even for some people.
This phenomenon is unique to the US, so if cicadas sing in your backyard, enjoy it while it lasts.

Adapted from: https://www.dogonews.com/2021/3/16/15-us-states-are-about-to-get-inundated-with-billions-of-noisy-cicadas (last accessed on 21.04.2021).

Part Two

> In part two a reporter is carrying out a survey. You will hear this twice. Before listening, you will have 40 seconds to read the task. You now have 40 seconds to read the task. *(40 seconds break)*
> You are now going to hear the survey for the first time. After a short break, you will hear the survey again. ◀

Survey: The royal family

Reporter: Good morning and welcome to today's phone-in. My name is Mark Dennison and you're listening to BBC Radio Kent. Our subject this morning is the British royal family. We're looking forward to hearing what you think about the Queen and other royal family members. Ah, here's our first caller.

Jeanette: Good morning, my name is Jeanette. I'm very critical of the royal family. I don't think they do enough for the money they get from the government. They live for free in fancy palaces and some members of the royal family are given their flashy clothes by designers. I also think that too much news time is taken up with trivial royal stories, about the Queen's dogs for example, when there is more important news.

Irene: My name is Irene and I disagree. I think the royal family does a lot of good. Let's face it, there are a lot of depressing things going on in the world right now and I think the royals bring some glamour and sparkle into our lives. Did you not see that photo last week of Prince George and Princess Charlotte in their school uniforms? They looked so cute!

Dominic: Hi, it's Dominic here. It doesn't matter whether you love or hate the royal family, they're here to stay. They are a part of our history and define us as a nation. Any seven-year-old in Britain can tell you that Henry VIII had six wives! The royal family represents stability and gives us a sense of identity. Just think of the Queen's speeches during the corona pandemic.

Leo: Good morning, my name is Leo. You may be surprised to know that the members of the royal family work very hard. Prince Charles, for example, attended 146 events last year on 141 working days. And the Queen, who is 95, attended 130 events. The work they do for charities is essential. Prince Charles is president of the British Red Cross Society, for example. This is just one of the 500 charities or organizations the Prince supports.

Alice: Hello there, my name is Alice. The British tax payers pay for the royal family. Last year they got 82 million pounds. This is obviously a lot of money, but at the end of the day, it was £ 1.24 per person in the UK. So, not giving them this money anymore doesn't make the ordinary man any richer.

Henry: My name is Henry and believe me, the rest of Europe would love to have a royal family like ours. A royal wedding or the birth of a baby prince or princess makes the best news. This interest in the royal family generates a lot of money and jobs. Over 2.7 million tourists visited Buckingham Palace and Windsor Castle last year, bringing in more than 550 million pounds.

Dave: Alright? It's Dave here. I think the royals are pretty harmless and they don't have any power. Although the Queen is the head of state, she does not run the country, she is not even allowed to say publicly what she thinks about the political decisions the government makes. They are allowed to support football teams, though. The Queen is an Arsenal fan and Prince William supports Aston Villa.

Reporter: What's your opinion on the royal family? Keep your calls coming!

Adapted from: https://www.historyextra.com/period/modern/why-royal-family-exist-guide-arguments-why-should-be-abolished-republicanism/ (last accessed on 21.04.2021).

Part Three

In part three you will hear an interview. You will hear the interview twice. Before listening to the interview, you will have 30 seconds to read the task. You now have 30 seconds to read the task.

(30 seconds break) You are now going to hear the interview for the first time. After a short break, you will hear the interview again. ◀

Interview: Food waste

Reporter: Today on the programme *Cleaner, greener planet*, our topic is food waste. Do you know that food waste causes just as much damage worldwide as plastic waste? Joining me in the studio is Julian Musgrove, who works for the UK Food Group. Good morning, Julian.

Julian: Good morning.

Reporter: Tell me, Julian. Why is throwing away food such a problem for the planet?

Julian: Well, it's not just the food we waste when we throw it away, but also the energy that has been used to produce it, process it and transport it. For example, the amount of water needed to produce one orange is 80 litres. One apple needs an average of 125 litres of water. The numbers with meat are even more shocking. For just one kilogramme of beef, you need 15,400 litres of water.

Reporter: Wow, that is surprising!

Julian: Yes, and it's not just a question of the energy needed to produce food. Food waste also produces the dangerous greenhouse gas methane. This gas is responsible for warming the planet. In the UK alone, the food we throw away creates 20 million tonnes of greenhouse gas, which is the same as the pollution from 3.5 million cars.

Reporter: But where does all the food waste come from?

Julian: In the UK, most food waste comes from our homes. Of the 10.2 million tonnes of food wasted, 7.1 million tonnes is from households. What is most worrying is that 5 million tonnes of this food is still edible.

Reporter: But some food waste is unavoidable. What about potato peelings, old teabags and egg shells? We can't eat those.

Julian: No, of course not. But we can use this food waste to create energy. For example, if your food waste is recycled properly, it is put into a tank without oxygen and then it is broken down by micro-organisms. This process produces a biogas which can generate electricity. The energy created by recycling one banana skin can fully charge a smart phone twice!

Reporter: Wow! So how can we reduce our food waste at home?

Julian: I recommend that you write a meal plan for the week and only buy what you need. People also need to understand the difference between 'use-by' dates and 'best-before' dates. 'Use-by' is about safety and food isn't safe to eat after this date. 'Best-before' is about quality. Foods are safe to eat after this date.

Reporter: When I cook at home, we often cook too much and then you end up throwing the rest away. What can we do about this?

Julian: Either eat it the following day or freeze it for a future meal. Most foods can be frozen – bread, if you slice it first, cheese and even eggs if you crack and beat them first.

Reporter: I often ask myself what happens to the food that is not sold in supermarkets. Is that thrown away too?

Julian: Not always. Some supermarkets donate unsold food to charities. The supermarket Tesco for example works with local charities which then pick up the surplus food and distribute it at food banks. In France, it is actually illegal for supermarkets to throw away unused food. They have to donate it.

Reporter: That is a very sensible law! Julian, thank you for coming on *Cleaner, greener planet* today and talking to us about this important topic.

Julian: It's a pleasure.

Adapted from: https://www.which.co.uk/news/2019/06/three-food-waste-facts-everyone-needs-to-know/ (last accessed on 25.02.2021).

You may now continue with the rest of the exam. Good luck!

A Listening Comprehension

Part One

Listen to the news items and tick (✓) the right statements.
There is only one possible answer per statement.

News Item 1: Famous auctions   4 pts.

a) MGM Studios started selling famous items from films
   - [ ] in 2014.
   - [ ] to save money.
   - [ ] to Hollywood stars.

b) At one sale, a weapon from *The Lord of the Rings* made
   - [ ] $510,000.
   - [ ] $660,000.
   - [ ] $256,000.

c) In the book *The Wizard of Oz*, Dorothy's shoes were originally
   - [ ] silver.
   - [ ] yellow.
   - [ ] red.

d) In 2020, a gun used by James Bond was purchased by
   - [ ] Sean Connery.
   - [ ] Dr. P. Walther.
   - [ ] an unknown buyer.

News Item 2: Cicadas   4 pts.

a) The cicadas have been underground for ____ years.
   - [ ] 10
   - [ ] 17
   - [ ] 64

b) These insects will appear
   - [ ] when the air temperature is 17 °C.
   - [ ] at night-time.
   - [ ] when it is rainy and windy.

c) The female cicadas lay their eggs
   - [ ] on trees.
   - [ ] underground.
   - [ ] at the end of the summer.

d) At the end of their lives, cicadas
   - [ ] feed on plant roots.
   - [ ] burrow into the soil.
   - [ ] are eaten by other animals.

Part Two

Survey: The royal family

*Listen to these people talking about the British royal family.
Who thinks what? Write the correct letters in the chart.
Be careful – there is one statement more than you need.*

7 pts.

A Britain benefits from tourism thanks to the royal family.

B The royals are financed by the government. I don't think they deserve it.

C The Queen's dogs are always in the news. She does great charity work for the Battersea Dogs and Cats Home.

D The charity work the royals do is so important.

E They're a part of our culture and identity.

F It's true that the Queen is head of state, but she doesn't exactly rule the country.

G To the man in the street, it makes no financial difference if the state finances the royal family or not.

H The royal family distracts us from the sad things in life.

Jeanette	Irene	Dominic	Leo	Alice	Henry	Dave

Part Three

Interview: Food waste

Listen to the interview and write down the information needed.
Fill in only one detail per box.

10 pts.

who Julian works for	
amount of water needed to grow one apple	
what food waste produces	
where the majority of UK food waste comes from	
positive effect of food waste if properly recycled	
what you can do with the energy generated from one banana skin	
one tip to reduce food waste at home	
what a 'use-by' date means	
how you freeze eggs	
what some supermarkets do with unsold food	

B Reading Comprehension

1. **"Go, Captain Tom!"**

    ❶ It was a rare piece of good news for a country gripped by a deadly disease which had claimed the lives of thousands of people. Encouraged by his daughter Hannah, Thomas Moore raised nearly £40 million for Britain's National Health Service (NHS) *Charities Together*. His challenge of walking 100 laps around his 25-metre garden started in April 2020 during the Covid-19 pandemic. At that time, he was 99 years old and wanted to complete 100 laps of his garden by Thursday, April 16th – a fortnight before his 100th birthday on April 30th. Captain Thomas Moore had dreamed of collecting £1,000. Instead, he raised tens of millions of pounds at the beginning of the pandemic.

    ❷ Thomas Moore had an eventful life. As early as 1940, aged just 20 years old, he wanted to serve the British army to fight in World War Two. So, he signed up as an officer in a regiment and was sent to Cornwall to defend the coast from a German invasion. After being selected for officer training, Tom quickly rose through the ranks to captain. He later said about the war, "I don't consider myself a hero, and at the end of the war I had survived virtually unharmed and realised I'd been one of the lucky ones. I hope we don't have any more wars because they are fruitless things."

    ❸ Thomas Moore was born in West Yorkshire and grew up with his father, who built houses, and his mother, a head teacher. He was educated at Keighley Grammar School before training as a civil engineer. In 1969, he married his wife Pamela and they had two daughters. After his wife had died in 2006, he moved to Bedfordshire and lived with his daughter Hannah and her family. "Tom's tale is one full of twists, turns and monumental moments in our British history", his daughter said, explaining why he simply could not sit back and do nothing when the nation was put under lockdown.

    ❹ When Captain Moore moved to Bedfordshire, he continued to lead a full life. Then, he had various medical problems and received intensive care and treatment in hospital. Inspired by that, he wanted to give something back to the NHS in its fight against the coronavirus. It was important for him to keep the attention focused solely on the charities which needed support. So he said, "When you think of who it is all for – all those brave and super doctors and nurses we have got – I think they deserve every penny.

    ❺ Captain Tom's story made international headlines across the globe. He also released a charity single, "You'll never walk alone". It reached number one in the charts, making him the oldest artist ever to have a UK number one single. In May 2020, at the age of 100, Captain Tom Moore was given a knighthood by Queen Elizabeth II. But in January 2021, he was diagnosed with pneumonia and treated in hospital. Later, he tested positive for the coronavirus and died on February 2nd, 2021. One day after his death, church bells and fireworks went off to honour the man who captured hearts around the world. People across the United Kingdom paid their respects to him by clapping Sir Captain Thomas Moore at the same time.

https://people.com/human-interest/uk-honors-captain-sir-tom-moore-after-his-death-by-clapping-across-the-nation/
https://www.bbc.co.uk/newsround/52277760
https://abcnews.go.com/International/100-year-veteran-captain-tom-knighted-fundraising-heroics/story?id=70784142
https://www.telegraph.co.uk/news/2020/05/19/sir-tom-moore-100-year-old-fundraising-veteran-given-knighthood/
https://www.cbsnews.com/news/captain-tom-moore-knighted-queen-elizabeth/
https://www.dailymail.co.uk/news/article-8225119/How-Captain-Tom-Moore-global-superstar.html
https://www.the-sun.com/news/1758477/captain-tom-moore-remembrance-day/
https://www.optimistdaily.com/2020/05/captain-tom-moore-knighted-for-his-inspiring-fundraising-campaign/
https://metro.co.uk/2020/04/16/tom-moore-story-behind-14000000-nhs-legend-12565964/
https://www.army.mod.uk/people/leave-well/service-leavers-veterans/army-skills/captain-sir-tom-moore/
https://abcnews.go.com/Entertainment/wireStory/queen-makes-veteran-knight-100-kneeling-required-71841800
https://www.smoothradio.com/news/entertainment/where-does-captain-tom-moore-live-daughter
(alle abgerufen am 12. 07. 2021, adaptiert)

Match the five correct headings to each part of the text (1–5).
Be careful – there are two headings more than you need. 5 pts.

A	GRIPPED BY THE PANDEMIC
B	GRATITUDE TOWARDS MEDICAL STAFF
C	GETTING FAME AND HONOUR
D	MILITARY CAREER
E	FIGHTING ABROAD
F	CHALLENGE TO RAISE MONEY
G	FAMILY LIFE

part of the text	❶	❷	❸	❹	❺
heading					

2. Soccer

Evidence of organized football games in Greece, Rome and China goes back more than 2,000 years, but historians have no idea how these games were played. However, the birthplace of modern soccer is Britain, both England and Scotland.

All modern forms of the game have their roots in the "folk football" which was played as early as in the 14th and 15th centuries. The sport of folk football, in former times also called "mob football", developed from other games. They were usually played around Easter and may have had their origins in pre-Christian customs to celebrate the return of spring. The games were played with a minimum of rules and were far more violent, more related to rugby in many respects. Images discovered from this period also seem to suggest that there was a huge number of players who could move the ball by any means necessary, including with their hands.

Villages competed against villages, kicking, throwing, and carrying a wooden or leather ball across fields and over streams, through narrow gateways and narrower streets. Everyone was involved – men and women, adults and children, rich and poor. These games involved full body contact and often turned bloody. The chaotic contest ended when a particularly robust or skillful villager managed to get the ball into the opposing village's goal.

In Ashbourne in Derbyshire, this kind of rough game has survived virtually non-stop. In 1878, the police attempted to forbid the game, but that only led to violent clashes. This form of the game is still popular and is a tourist attraction in Ashbourne today.

In medieval times in England, the game was so much loved by the common people that it was very often banned. Kings and Queens wanted their men to improve their fighting skills instead of playing ball.

At the beginning of the 19th century, football was played in prestigious schools like Eton or other public schools. When the privileged graduates of these schools went on to Oxford and Cambridge, none of them was ready to play by the rules of someone else's school because each school had its own variations. To unify the game, the original Cambridge Rules were written down by students in 1848. This was the first attempt to distance football from its shared roots with rugby and to form a distinct identity as soccer.

Modern football originated during the second half of the 19th century in Britain. Industrial workers increasingly had Saturday afternoons off, which was new for the people who worked. So many began to watch and play the exciting game of football.

Later in 1863, the Football Association (FA) was formed and its rules dominated the game from now on. Professionalism came to soccer as early as 1885, although players could only expect a wage of around one pound per week, which is a world away from today's fabulous fees. In 1869, touching the ball with your hands was forbidden. In the 1880s, students at Oxford University created a slang word for the word "association". They shortened it to "SOC" and added "ER", so the word "soccer" was finally created.

https://www.bbc.co.uk/bitesize/guides/zqvf39q/revision/1
https://www.britannica.com/sports/football-the-games#ref885261
https://myworldsoccer.com/a-broad-history-of-english-football/
https://www.information-britain.co.uk/sporthistory/entry/Football/
http://www.nads.org.uk/football-history/history-of-football-in-england
https://www.football-stadiums.co.uk/articles/folk-football/
http://www.homeoffootball.net/wp-content/uploads/2020/03/SHOF-final_compressed.pdf
https://www.englisch-hilfen.de/en/words/football_soccer1.htm
http://www.sportingsheffield.com/home-of-football/)
(alle abgerufen am 12. 07. 2021, adaptiert)

Abschlussprüfung Englisch 2022

Tick (✓) the right statement. There is only one possible answer per statement. 10 pts.

a) The birthplace of soccer as we know it today is
- [ ] Britain.
- [ ] China.
- [ ] Rome.
- [ ] Greece.

b) In former times, folk football was played to
- [ ] develop ball games.
- [ ] develop ball rules.
- [ ] celebrate special customs.
- [ ] celebrate the new season.

c) Images suggest that the games were played
- [ ] exactly like rugby.
- [ ] with the hands only.
- [ ] with all needed means.
- [ ] by only a small number of players.

d) During the competition, many people
- [ ] scored goals for their villages.
- [ ] left the chaotic contest.
- [ ] were injured.
- [ ] managed to be clever.

e) _____ attempted to abolish the game in Ashbourne.
- [ ] Derbyshire
- [ ] The police
- [ ] Fierce clashes
- [ ] Some tourists

f) Monarchs wanted to _____ their men's fighting techniques.
- [ ] increase
- [ ] prove
- [ ] show
- [ ] decrease

E 2022-10

g) At respected schools, students played football according to ____ rules.
- [ ] ordinary
- [ ] varying
- [ ] noble
- [ ] privileged

h) With the Cambridge Rules, football became ____ rugby.
- [ ] connected to
- [ ] similar to
- [ ] different from
- [ ] equal to

i) Many factory workers could
- [ ] play football all Saturday.
- [ ] attend matches every afternoon.
- [ ] be kept from work by playing the exciting game.
- [ ] play football in the afternoon at weekends.

k) The word soccer was formed by
- [ ] adding one letter to a word.
- [ ] shortening two words.
- [ ] using a shortened form of a letter.
- [ ] shortening letters of a word and adding others.

3. Preparing for a date

In the following extract, Trevor, a young black South African, is trying to improve his looks because he has a date for the school dance. His friend Bongani is helping him.

Bongani […] found out I had a date, and he made it his mission to give me a makeover. "You need to up your game," he said. "You cannot go to the dance looking the way you look – for her sake, not yours. Let's go shopping."

I went to my mom and begged her to give me money to buy something to wear for the dance. She finally relented and gave me 2,000 rand[1], for one outfit. It was the most money she'd ever given me for anything in my life. I told Bongani how much I had to spend, and he said we'd make it work. The trick to looking rich, he told me, is to have one expensive item, and for the rest of the things you get basic, good-looking quality stuff. […] He took me shopping and we bought a calf-length black leather jacket, which would look ridiculous today but at the time […] was very cool. That alone cost 1,200 rand. Then we finished the outfit with a pair of simple black pants, suede square-toed shoes, and a cream-white knitted sweater.

Once we had the outfit, Bongani took a long look at my enormous Afro. […] "We need to fix that fucking hair," Bongani said.

"What do you mean?" I said. "This is just my hair."

"No, we *have* to do something."

Bongani lived in Alexandra. He dragged me there, and we went to talk to some girls from his street who were hanging out on the corner. "What would you do with this guy's hair?" he asked them.

The girls looked me over.

"He has so much," one of them said. "Why doesn't he cornrow[2] it?"

"Shit, yeah," they said. "That's great!"

I said, "What? Cornrows? No!"

"No, no," they said. "Do it."

Bongani dragged me to a hair salon down the street. We went in and sat down. The woman touched my hair, shook her head, and turned to Bongani.

"I can't work with this sheep," she said. "You have to do something about this."

"What do we need to do?"

"You have to relax it. I don't do that here."

"Okay."

Bongani dragged me to a second salon. I sat down in the chair, and the woman took my hair and started painting this creamy white stuff in it. She was wearing rubber gloves to keep this chemical relaxer off her own skin, which should have been my first clue that maybe this wasn't such a great idea. [...] What I didn't know is that the chemical doesn't really start to burn until it's being rinsed out. I felt like someone was pouring liquid fire onto my head. When I was done I had patches of acid burns all over my scalp. I was the only man in the salon; it was all women. It was a window into what women experience to look good on a regular basis. *Why would they ever do this?*, I thought. *This is horrible.* But it worked. My hair was completely straight. [...]

Bongani then dragged me back to the first salon, and the woman agreed to cornrow my hair. She worked slowly. It took six hours. Finally she said, "Okay, you can look in the mirror." She turned me around in the chair and I looked in the mirror and ... I had never seen myself like that before. [...]

Everyone in my family loved it. They all thought it looked great. My mom did tease [...] me, though.

"It's very well done," she said, "but it is way too pretty. You do look like a girl."

Trevor Noah: *Born a crime*, Spiegel & Grau: New York 2016, S. 170–173

1 rand = currency in South Africa
2 cornrow = *here:* a special hair style

Answer the questions.

a) Why does Trevor need a makeover? 1 pt.

b) How does Trevor's mum help him with the makeover? 1 pt.

c) What is Bongani's tip to make yourself look rich? 1 pt.

d) What special clothing do Trevor and Bongani buy? (Name two details.) 2 pts.

e) Who does Bongani talk to first about Trevor's hair? 1 pt.

f) Why can't the woman in the first salon work with Trevor's hair? 1 pt.

g) How does Trevor's mum tease him? 1 pt.

You cannot find the answers to the following questions directly in the text:

h) Why does Trevor's mum give him more money than ever before? 1 pt.

i) After his experience in the second salon, Trevor makes a discovery about women. What is it? 1 pt.

C Use of Language

1. Mediation

Hitchhiking USA

14 pts.

Du bist mit deinen Eltern auf einer Autoreise in den Vereinigten Staaten unterwegs. Ihr nehmt einen Anhalter mit.
Vermittle zwischen Jason, dem Anhalter, und deinen Eltern. Ergänze den folgenden Dialog mit den wichtigsten Informationen in der jeweils geforderten Sprache.

Jason: Thanks a lot for giving me a lift. I really appreciate it. It's pretty hot out there today and I had been waiting for about two hours already.

Du [Deutsch]: _____ 2 pts.

_____

Mutter: Keine Ursache! Ich bin, als ich jünger war, auch per Anhalter durch halb Europa gefahren. Allerdings dachte ich immer, dass das in den USA illegal ist. Frag ihn doch bitte mal danach.

Du [Englisch]: _____ 1 pt.

_____

Jason: Yes and no. It's illegal to stand on the side of a major highway and stop cars because it is a danger to other drivers on the road. However, standing at the entrance before a highway is legal in most states.

Du [Deutsch]: _____ 2 pts.

_____

Vater: Also, ich würde das niemals machen. Man liest so viel über die Gefahren und man weiß nie, wer einen da mitnimmt. Denkt er nicht, dass es gefährlich ist?

Du [Englisch]: _____ 1 pt.

_____

Jason: Before I started, I was told numerous times that I would have to be careful. Based on my own experience, I can say that you don't have to worry too much. Most of the people I met were friendly, fascinating and full of entertaining stories.

Du [Deutsch]: _____ 2 pts.

_____

Vater: Na, das klingt jetzt aber fast zu schön, um wahr zu sein. Er muss doch sicher einiges beachten, damit er sicher unterwegs ist. Frag ihn doch mal nach den wichtigsten Sicherheitsregeln, die er beachtet.

Du [Englisch]: _____ 1 pt.

_____

Jason: Well, you have to be prepared for everything, really. I think it's important to look confident, so I always look drivers in the eye and smile as they pass. Also, I don't get into every car that stops for me – I trust my instincts. Most importantly, I always snap a quick photo of the back of the car and send it to my twitter account.

Du [Deutsch]: _____ 2 pts.

_____

_____

Mutter: Das ist mir gerade alles viel zu ernst hier! Ich habe damals auch nur tolle Menschen getroffen und die lustigsten Sachen erlebt. Frage ihn bitte, was bisher sein lustigstes Erlebnis war.

Du [Englisch]: _____ 1 pt.

_____

Jason: Oh my gosh, that was only two days ago. There was the cutest puppy ever, which I got to hold on my lap for the ride. There was, however, a catch to its cuteness. It was the first car trip for the puppy and she was feeling car sick: after a few bends on the road, the car filled with a disgusting smell. We stopped and checked her fur, but fortunately, they were just farts. We had to ride the rest of the way with the windows down …

Du [Deutsch]: _____ 2 pts.

_____

_____

Alle: Ha, ha, ha …

2. Words and structures

Read the text, then tick (✓) the correct words.   11 pts.

Record trip to Mount Everest summit

Many have already successfully climbed Mount Everest, the highest mountain on our planet. One of them has recently set a new record: Kami Rita, a Sherpa guide, _1_ the summit for the 25th time, setting a new record for the most ascents of the _2_ highest peak.

He was part of the first group of climbers to reach the summit this year. They _3_ fixing the ropes on the icy route, so that hundreds of other climbers could attempt to reach the peak later this month. Kami, 51, first climbed Everest _4_ 1994 and has been making the trip nearly every year since then. He is one of many Sherpa guides _5_ experience and skills are essential _6_ the safety on the mountain. Each year, hundreds of climbers _7_ to Nepal seeking to successfully stand on top of the 8848-metre mountain.

Forty-three teams have permission to climb Everest during this year's spring climbing season and will be _8_ by about 400 Nepalese guides.

Each May, there are usually only a _9_ periods of good weather at the summit during which climbers can try to reach the peak.

Sherpas are a native people from the Himalayas. Traditionally, they believe that the summits of mountains are where gods live and they should be admired _10_ far away rather than conquered. Before summiting a mountain, Sherpas perform a prayer and flag ceremony called Puja, which is a _11_ of paying respect to the gods of the mountain.

https://www.kidsnews.com.au/humanities/sherpa-kami-summits-everest-for-record-25th-time/news-story/3318e5eb7e963056558912b4aad361a 0 (abgerufen am 20. 05. 2021, adaptiert).

1. ☐ reaches ☐ has reached ☐ will reach ☐ didn't reach	2. ☐ worlds ☐ world ☐ worlds' ☐ world's	3. ☐ were ☐ was ☐ will ☐ want	4. ☐ on ☐ at ☐ in ☐ for
5. ☐ whose ☐ who ☐ who's ☐ what	6. ☐ at ☐ with ☐ for ☐ about	7. ☐ head ☐ tail ☐ arm ☐ leg	8. ☐ assist ☐ assists ☐ assisting ☐ assisted
9. ☐ rarely ☐ few ☐ little ☐ small	10. ☐ from ☐ by ☐ at ☐ with	11. ☐ street ☐ path ☐ alley ☐ way	

D Text Production

Choose one of the following tasks and write about 150 words.
Count your words and write the number at the end of the text.

25 pts.

What is the story behind the picture?

Imagine this photo is the object of a creative writing competition and you decide to enter.

Write a text and include at least four of the following aspects:
- Who are they?
- Where are they?
- What happened before?
- How do they feel?
- What will happen next?

or

What is the story behind the picture?

Imagine this photo is the object of a creative writing competition and you decide to enter.

Write a text and include at least four of the following aspects:
- Who are they?
- Where are they?
- What happened before?
- How do they feel?
- What will happen next?

Simon Hall / Twitter

or

The school of the future

In a project, a university is asking pupils to submit ideas for the school of the future. You decide to take part.

Write a text and include at least four of the following aspects:
- What does the school of the future look like?
- How do the pupils learn?
- Where do the pupils learn?
- Who does the teaching?
- What makes the school of the future better than today's school?

Hessen Realschule – Englisch
Jahrgang 2023

Um dir die Prüfung 2023 schnellstmöglich zur Verfügung stellen zu können, bringen wir sie in digitaler Form heraus.

Sobald die Original-Prüfungsaufgaben 2023 freigegeben sind, können sie als PDF auf der Plattform **MyStark** heruntergeladen werden (Zugangscode vgl. Umschlaginnenseite).

Aktuelle Prüfung

www.stark-verlag.de/mystark